Frederick Law Olmsted, Sr.

Founder of Landscape Architecture in America

Frederick Law Olmsted, Sr.

Founder of Landscape Architecture in America

JULIUS GY. FABOS, GORDON T. MILDE, &

V. MICHAEL WEINMAYR

THE UNIVERSITY OF MASSACHUSETTS PRESS

To the members of the American Society of Landscape Architects

Preface

The original impetus for this book was a suggestion by Sidney N. Shurcliff, Trustee of the American Society of Landscape Architects; at his instigation, the Society in 1963 formed a committee to develop a suitable tribute to Frederick Law Olmsted, Sr. in celebration of the centennial year of the first use of the term "landscape architect." This committee turned for advice to Norman T. Newton, Professor of Landscape Architecture at Harvard University. He favored the idea of an exhibition about Olmsted's life and work; the burden of direction, compilation, and production was immediately assumed by several of his pupils. Completed in 1964, the exhibition went on national tour. This book represents our determination to give the collected graphic materials a more permanent form.

The inspiration of Olmsted brought the aid of students and professional designers for both the exhibition and the book. Of inestimable help to the editors were both the ready access granted to the public and private files of Olmsted's work and the interested encouragement of other members of the Departments of Landscape Architecture at Harvard University and the University of Massachusetts. We would like to thank in particular: Charles Harris, Hideo Sasaki, Norman Newton, Sidney Shurcliff, Albert Fein, Thomas McNulty, José Luis Sert, Dorothea K. Harrison, Henry Hope Reed, Charles W. Eliot, William B. Marquis, and the firm of Olmsted Associates, Inc. Additional material has been provided by Harvey Wish, Grady Clay, John O. Simonds, Lewis Mumford, Garrett Eckbo, Stewart Udall, and Ervin Zube; some of their many comments have been incorporated in our text.

Much credit belongs to the members of the exhibition team who, with the authors, did all the preliminary research for this book at Harvard University.

These workers include John Furlong, Charles Fryling, Terry Schnadelbach, Slamet Wirasondjaja, and Joseph Volpe. Particular thanks are due to William Tishler, who also later provided photographs of Olmsted's Riverside development specifically for this book. Special thanks are also due to Michael Laurie, who studied the later development of Stanford University for the purposes of this book.

Our own determination to present a worthy tribute to Frederick Law Olmsted, Sr. was reinforced by the support of these individuals. The virtues of this volume are the result of constructive criticism from these sources; the faults, needless to say, are our own.

Julius Gy. Fabos
Gordon T. Milde
V. Michael Weinmayr

The authors wish to acknowledge the support and cooperation of the Hubbard Educational Trust, and to express their gratitude to Albert Fein for calling their attention to several errors which have been corrected in this second printing. The authors wish to acknowledge as well their considerable debt to Frederick Law Olmsted, Landscape Architect: Forty Years of Landscape Architecture, *from which several quotations in the captions were taken.*

Contents

Illustrations

Frederick Law Olmsted, Sr.

Founder of Landscape Architecture in America

Introduction

The history of landscape architecture as a profession in America begins with Central Park, New York, begun in 1857 and completed in 1863. Before this project American cities included no large, informal recreation spaces as part of their regular plan of development. State and national parks were unknown. Campus, urban, and community design existed as secondary aspects of architecture, engineering, or surveying. After the success of Central Park, however, every major American city began to imitate New York's example. The demand for parks created a profession of men skilled in meeting the diverse problems of engineering, horticulture, and design. In a short time this profession expanded to include services previously regarded as less important adjuncts to other disciplines.

As the man who helped design Central Park, supervised its construction, and worked and trained others to fill the demand which Central Park created, Frederick Law Olmsted, Sr. was, simply, the founder of the profession of landscape architecture in America. With his partner, Calvert Vaux, he was responsible for the inclusion of large landscaped parks and planned natural preserves in America's development after 1863. With Vaux, and later in independent practice, Olmsted trained the majority of designers and planners who were to shape the country's physical growth throughout the late nineteenth century.

The story of Olmsted's achievement is in part the history of America's growth from a rural republic to an industrial democracy. When Olmsted was born in 1822, America was a harmonious rural nation. Over ninety percent of her ten million citizens lived on farms or in villages of less than eight thousand residents. The three largest cities of the nation were New York (123,000 residents), Philadelphia (113,000), and Baltimore (63,000). None of these urban areas was extensively developed more than two miles from its commercial center. The great majority of America's population lived on intimate terms with nature; the people's work, their social habits, their comforts, and their very health were regulated by the cycle of the passing seasons. Those city dwellers liberated from the toil of farms still found the pleasures of domesticated nature within an hour's walk from town.

When Olmsted died in 1903, this world was gone. New York had grown to have almost four million residents; the next largest city, Chicago (1.7 million), had existed only as a trading post in 1822. Twenty-five million citizens, one-third of the nation, lived in cities. Many lived in slums as bad as any on the face of the globe. (A trend had developed that will see seventy percent of America's population living in urban areas by 1970.) In the lots and alleys of Boston's North End, New York's Five Points, and San Francisco's Chinatown, the slum resident found access to nature and open space limited to what planning had saved from the inexorable spread of urban development.

When Olmsted, aged twelve, rode with his father on long trips through New England, in 1834, there were still many acres of virgin forest in the region. The fastest form of bulk transportation, when available, was paddle-wheel steamer or horse-drawn canal boat. Slow travel limited exploitation of natural resources. The western borders of America were still those of the Louisiana Purchase; Southern sentiment echoed Thomas Jefferson's thought, in 1803, that it might take centuries to colonize the existing frontier.

By 1903 the frontier was officially closed. America's borders extended to the Pacific, and a huge network of railroads tied the East to the Plains and to California. The forests of the Rocky Mountains and the Pacific Northwest were open to exploitation. New England, denuded of her virgin timber and with new pine seedlings growing in her abandoned pastures, was in the twilight of her pastoral age. Throughout the region thousands of empty cellarholes marked the emigration of Eastern farmers to the Middle West. Soon New England textile mills

FREDERICK LAW OLMSTED, SR., ca. 1860–65
[Olmsted Office Portfolio]

[5]

would begin their passage to a South still crippled by the disastrous effects of the Civil War and the remnants of a slave economy.

Nationally, America had passed from an aristocracy and the Virginia Dynasty through Jacksonian Democracy to the oligarchy of the Gilded Age. On a local level town meetings and representative democracy yielded to block voting, ward politics, and the rule of the political boss.

To establish the values of nature in such an age of growth required an exceptional man. Olmsted's personal history is noteworthy, even in a century that produced Abraham Lincoln, Joseph Smith, and Samuel F. B. Morse.

Olmsted never graduated from any grammar school or college; his earliest tutors were Connecticut clergymen in a scattering of boarding homes and one-room schoolhouses. When it came time to choose a calling at sixteen, he was in turn a surveyor, part-time Yale student, bookkeeper, and sailor. In 1847, he established a widely acclaimed model farm on Staten Island with parental funds. Neglected for journalism, publishing, and long trips about the country, it fell to ruin by 1860. With friends he assumed control of a New York publishing firm in 1855; by 1856 it was bankrupt. Until well into his thirties he received substantial and necessary financial support from his father, whose occasional irascible letters did little to ease his peace of mind. Landscape architecture was adopted by chance, abandoned for public health, and only reluctantly resumed.

Seldom in any endeavor did he see his own ideal of perfection realized, although he came closer than most men. Perhaps his uncompromising idealism explains the irritation with the shortcomings of his associates which is reflected in his writings. Throughout his life he was plagued with sensitive nerves, a disability which eventually led him to do much of his work in the quiet night hours when most of the world had retired. His declining years were spent as a patient at Mc-Lean's Institute (the grounds of which had been his first Boston commission).

Incidental work in the course of his life included authorship of the definitive work on the ante-bellum South, establishment of what later became the American Red Cross, and co-founding of *The Nation*.

FREDERICK LAW OLMSTED, SR.
*At the time of the
construction of Central Park
[Olmsted Office Portfolio]*

CALVERT VAUX, ca. 1860
*Olmsted's friend and partner
throughout the major part
of his career
[Olmsted Office Portfolio]*

We can see in retrospect that most of the training of Olmsted's early life added to his skill as a landscape architect. He was a man who approached his profession indirectly and who attained his special success with a collection of skills not usually defined as part of the curriculum.

Olmsted's first major venture, as an experimental farmer, ultimately led to his career as a journalist. Articles he wrote about his experiments on Staten Island brought him into correspondence with such men as William Cullen Bryant and the American landscape gardener and architect Andrew Jackson Downing. His prominence as a writer began with publication of *Walks and Talks of an American Farmer in England* (1852), the description of a walking tour to study British agriculture. One of the major by-products of this tour was a visit to "People's Park" in Birkenhead, England; here Olmsted was introduced to his first example of a large public park set aside for the enjoyment of all citizens.

Olmsted's growing reputation as a writer and agriculturalist gained for him a commission from the New York *Times* to travel in the South and report on economic and social conditions. The experience of his trips (beginning in 1852) and the contents of several books and innumerable dispatches were ultimately distilled into *The Cotton Kingdom* (2 vols., 1861). In this work Olmsted presented a graphic picture of conditions in the South and analyzed the lack of incentive for personal labor and industrial development that were the fundamental weaknesses of a slave-centered economy. His writings remain the definitive critique of pre-war plantation society. In later years, despite professional commitments, he continued to pour forth articles, particularly for *The Nation*.

In 1857, endorsed by many notables familiar with his work, he was appointed superintendent in charge of construction of New York's Central Park. And the man who was to become the founder of the twin disciplines of landscape architecture and city planning met the project which was to become the most conspicuous and enduring monument to his achievement in these disciplines. Except for a distinguished two-year term of service (1861–1863) during the Civil War as secretary of the United States Sanitary Commission, the predecessor of the

FREDERICK LAW OLMSTED, SR., ca. 1860–1870
Taken in Paris during one of his many trips to Europe
[Olmsted Office Portfolio]

[9]

American Red Cross, Olmsted was to devote the remainder of his life to landscape architecture.

As he stood, in 1857, on the threshold of his career as a planner and channeler of the growth of the bustling, changing American nation, Olmsted could be fairly described as a romantic, a trained engineer, an experienced farmer, a cosmopolitan man, a sharp observer and social critic, an accomplished writer, a proven manager, and a man of understanding and compassion. This extraordinary combination of traits and abilities in conjunction with that quality that makes a man an artist was to enable Olmsted to design some of the most outstanding, constructive achievements of nineteenth-century America.

He had derived from his childhood experiences a romantic idealism which, like that of earlier nineteenth-century Americans, saw in unspoiled nature and the simple life a great force for the rehabilitation and rejuvenation of the human spirit enervated by the pressures of civilized life. To balance that idealism, he had gained from his training in civil engineering and surveying the discipline of practical experience—the ability to lay out and direct actual earth moving and construction, the knowledge of what the construction machinery of his age could do and of how long it would take at what cost to do a specific job. His years as an experimental farmer had developed his feeling for the land, for living plants, and for the union of the two in an organic whole. His extensive travels, both abroad and in his own country, had acquainted him with social and economic structures different from those of his native New England and developed his powers of critical observation. The outgrowth of these travels, his writings, gave him practice in the clear formulation and concise statement of his ideas.

It was no coincidence that the growth of landscape architecture as a profession closely paralleled America's industrial revolution, or that its founder was a jack-of-all-trades whose imagination was firmly rooted in ante-bellum America. The physical and social change of Olmsted's day produced a need for exceptional men to order the tempo of "progress." Just as commercial competition would develop a few titans whose goal was to eliminate industrial conflicts, so chaotic growth

FREDERICK LAW OLMSTED, SR., ca. 1890–95
[Olmsted Office Portfolio]

[11]

developed the need for a profession to order physical patterns of land use. Unlike America's Morgans or Vanderbilts, however, Olmsted and his associates found their first inspiration in the remembered forms of a past era. It was above all the physical pleasures and privileges of Jeffersonian America that Olmsted sought to bring intact into the industrial age.

For forty years, beginning with Central Park in 1858, Olmsted worked to create his own ideal of beauty for the benefit of millions. The result of his work was one of the most fortunate developments that shaped the face of America.

Olmsted's very adherence to the ideal of rural pleasures does not imply that he was simply a preservationist. The amount of spadework needed to create Central Park, as well as the number and variety of his undertakings, disproves this contention. Rather, Olmsted believed implicitly that a close association with natural beauty was one of the most necessary elements of human life. For the human spirit nature provided a psychological balm available nowhere else.

In holding this belief, Olmsted paralleled the preoccupations of the era in which he grew to manhood. It was a time when intellectual Americans had turned to nature for inspiration as an earlier age had turned to religion. Romanticists, inspired in part by Wordsworth and other Europeans, believed that man could find God by contemplating the "sublime" in nature. New England Transcendentalists, who flourished during the 1840's, argued that man's essential unity with God was reflected in his relation to the natural world around him. Beginning about 1825, artists such as the Hudson River painters filled the homes of their patrons with the natural splendors of the new world depicted on huge canvases. In poetry, William Cullen Bryant gained early fame for *Thanatopsis* and *To a Waterfowl*. In 1845, Thoreau began his two-year sojourn at Walden Pond. Those interested in the more domesticated beauties of nature found a spokesman in Andrew Jackson Downing; his works, which began appearing in 1841, encouraged a wide interest in landscape gardening for public buildings and estates. (It was Downing who, in 1850, brought to America as his partner Calvert Vaux, the English architect who later worked closely with Olmsted.)

Of the work of all the men of this era, Olmsted's is probably the most evident today. Downing died before his prime, in 1852, his major commission having been the landscaping of the Smithsonian Institute. Olmsted's physical creations provide for him an enduring monument; his parks are perhaps the most easily accessible survivals of nineteenth-century ideals in twentieth-century America.

In effect, Olmsted's was not a retreat from the growth of industrial America; it was a necessary corollary to that growth. Particularly in an age of rapid social and physical change, man needed to remind himself of a natural order that was permanent and of a beauty more subtle than that of bricks and mortar. It was this quality of life which Olmsted sought to create through his many parks and communities. Like Olmsted's writing, publishing, and Civil War hospital activities, landscape architecture provided a means for him to render a social service to help solve the problems of a changing nation.

Some of the traits which made Olmsted so great in his own time and a landmark for future generations include the following. First, Olmsted had a sense of the necessity for a balanced relationship between man and the natural world the antecedents for which lay in the pre-industrial America which he knew as a boy. Natural scenery, he wrote, exists "for the mind without fatigue and yet exercises it, tranquilizes it and yet enlivens it," thus refreshing the whole human system. The precept remains valid, however neglected, today.

Second, Olmsted's work showed an almost unbelievable amount of foresight. With a few other visionary men he designed for the day when the stone walls of Manhattan would crowd against its only large, open space. In his wilderness preserves he protected countless acres for future generations. Olmsted's suburban Riverside foresaw the modern need for bedroom communities joined to the city by pleasant approaches. Joining with America's most prominent designers in the Columbian Exhibition he executed a site plan which, if imitated, would provide for other American cities an environment to be enjoyed by all inhabitants.

One of Olmsted's more important traits was an ability to support his ideas in writing. He understood that an idea, no matter how well represented in graphic terms, would achieve a more lasting impact if it were expressed in words. His writing skill not only promoted his design ideas, but also served as a useful tool in fighting the political battles that plagued him throughout his involvement with municipal park administration.

Finally, in the execution of his projects, Olmsted showed a sensitivity to the potential of his site combined with a practical ability to supervise large problems and small details. Construction of Central Park's hills, ponds, and "natural" ledges required the movement of several million cubic yards of stone and earth, a project which Olmsted personally supervised. His knowledge of engineering enabled him to make Boston's Fens both a pleasure ground and an efficient container for a massive flood control system to serve the city. With such ability, Olmsted seldom found himself baffled by the requirements of a site. He used the nineteenth-century equivalent of the bulldozer, but his efforts invariably left the land more scenic than he had found it; there was never danger of his turning an open space into a featureless plain. In creating major areas of beauty throughout America, Olmsted established lasting precedents for its beautification at a critical point in our history.

The projects on the following pages suggest both the scope of Olmsted's talent and the wide range of activities to which he applied it. During his active career (1857–1895) his professional staff developed from a two-man collaboration in New York to a forty-man office in Boston (to which he had removed his practice in 1878).

In the course of Olmsted's career he and his associates worked on hundreds of major design projects. From these it is possible to describe only a few of the most important. (Additional major works are listed in Appendix I.) Olmsted's work strongly influenced the later scope of landscape architecture and planning. The following projects were chosen because they show the full range of his influence, because they represent his talent for innovation, and because they are among the projects in which he had the greatest success in carrying out his full intentions.

[14]

What artist so noble . . . as he who, with far-reaching conception of beauty and designing power, sketches the outlines, writes the colors, and directs the shadows of a picture so great that Nature shall be employed upon it for generations, before the work he has arranged for her shall realize his intentions.

FREDERICK LAW OLMSTED, SR.

Urban Parks

The success of Olmsted's design for Central Park launched him on his career as a landscape architect; today, the park is still America's best-known example of far-sighted planning. Its size and location, in America's largest city, are alone enough to ensure the park's prominence. It is the outstanding quality of Olmsted's design, however, which set the park apart as a landmark in American culture.

Rapid unplanned growth of the new world's great commercial centers had begun to make urban life intolerable by the 1850's. This was particularly true of New York, America's largest metropolis, which had a population of 700,000 by 1850. As at the present time, wealthier citizens feared the riots of the poor, and the specter of social revolution haunted the imagination of many of Olmsted's own associates. In 1857 a visitor wrote home that the newspapers reported a murder almost every day. In later years, Charles Loring Brace, a New Yorker, a social reformer, and an intimate friend of Olmsted since boyhood, writing of the revolution of 1872 in France, said that "there are just the same explosive elements beneath the surface of New York as of Paris." Recalling the draft riots of 1863, Brace observed: "Had another day of license been given the crowd, the attack would have been directed at the apparent wealth of the city—the banks, jeweler's shops, and rich private houses."

New York had more than tripled its population during the first half of the nineteenth century. As population, crowding, and poverty increased, open space and opportunities for rest and relaxation away from the pressures of the city decreased. The grid plan for New York's streets, laid down in 1811, included provisions for small urban parks. These plans were largely ignored during ensuing decades. Except for City Hall Square, The Battery (a former militia field), and a

[17]

few squares such as Madison Park, there were no places for outdoor public recreation. Acreage devoted to public open space actually decreased by fifty percent between 1800 and 1850, as residential squares were sold by the city or private proprietors for commercial use.

Civic figures, such as William Cullen Bryant and Andrew Jackson Downing, recognized the need for a park large enough to resist piecemeal destruction and to provide a rural contrast to the stone blocks of Manhattan. As early as 1844 Bryant proposed that some 500 acres be set aside for such a park. Initial discussion focused on two possible park sites—one at roughly the site of the present park and another bounded by Third Avenue and the East River from 66th to 75th Streets.

After much discussion and political infighting, the state legislature authorized, in 1853, the taking of 624 acres between 59th and 106th Streets for the initial tract. After more delay caused by friction between city and state governments the legislature appointed an independent Park Commission responsible to the governor. It was this commission that appointed Olmsted superintendent of construction and subsequently awarded the design competition prize to the plan anonymously submitted by Olmsted and Vaux under the title "Greensward."

Olmsted created, in Central Park, an area where urbanites could taste all the joys of rural life, including seclusion, without leaving the city. His plan included separation of through traffic by depressed roadways and provision for physical, aesthetic, and social enjoyment, without conflict, in different areas of the park. Olmsted was particularly concerned with the different types of recreation that open space made possible: the passive enjoyment of scenery that would give average citizens "certain kinds of refreshment of minds and nerves," the more active forms of physical recreation and sport absent elsewhere in Manhattan, and the pleasures of meeting friends in the pleasant surroundings provided by the formal atmosphere of the mall. His final plan made provision for all three pleasures.

Influenced by the man-made pastoral landscapes of England (particularly "People's Park" in Birkenhead), Olmsted designed his park as a series of open

URBAN CONDITIONS IN NEW YORK, ca. 1890
*Much of Olmsted's work was directed toward relieving such
crowding and providing areas where citizens could temporarily
escape from their surroundings*
[The Bettmann Archive]

and closing vistas, where the eye could be constantly refreshed by new scenes. To avoid the visual intrusion of cross-city movement he created sunken roadways that dropped the traffic below eye level and he attempted to screen out abutting buildings with plantings of trees. Specially-created ponds allowed the pleasures of boating and skating; trails meandering informally through the park above cross-city arteries provided exercise for the rider or hiker. For the more socially inclined, Olmsted designed the park's mall and fountain as focal points, where families could stroll, talk, or listen to band concerts. Informal arrangements of planting and segregation of activities, Olmsted felt, were the best way to create a man-made imitation of natural beauty.

Olmsted's achievement is all the more remarkable in view of the major problems which he and Vaux had to solve. Both as designer and superintendent of construction, Olmsted faced immense physical problems. At the time of his appointment the park site was swampy, brush-filled, littered with the debris of evicted squatters, crossed by dirt rights of way, and infested with goats. The presence of the Croton Reservoirs in the middle of the area precluded a wholly unified design. (Eventually it proved advisable to extend the upper park to 110th Street to add more space.) Draining, road-making, planting, brush-cutting, and digging artificial ponds were all necessary operations. During the course of his work Olmsted rearranged almost five million cubic yards of earth and rock to create his "pastoral" vistas; 114 miles of drainage pipe were used before the deceptively natural ponds and fields took their final shape.

In addition to his initial engineering problems Olmsted had to engage in running battles with politicians, professional associates, and lobbyists who wished to modify the construction or tamper with the administration of adequate maintenance. Throughout his career with the park Olmsted found it necessary to engage in active public lobbying in his own behalf, and ultimately New York itself found that it was perhaps easier to create a beautiful park than to ensure its responsible supervision.

At the time of Olmsted's resignation as supervisor, in 1863, the park was far from finished. Even before its completion, however, it was a major success. In 1862, its first year of operation, it attracted 25,000 visitors a day. Elegant families drove along its roads in carriages, children played hide-and-seek in the wilderness, and on winter evenings young men and women organized midnight skating parties on the frozen ponds.

Rehired in 1865 as landscape architect to the park, Olmsted's firm continued to advise on its development until 1870. At that time control of the park and its personnel shifted from the Park Commission to Boss Tweed who used this control to provide patronage jobs and ignored Olmsted and Vaux's advice on proper park maintenance. In protest, they resigned as consulting landscape architects. Public indignation forced their reappointment in 1871, but Olmsted was again discharged in 1878 by patronage-minded politicians who resented insistence on honest and competent administration.

Olmsted's pamphlet criticizing park administration (*Spoils of the Park*, 1882) suggests the problems that came to plague his project when it passed into municipal control—lack of adequate repair of drains, too little supervision by police, toleration of vandalism, and neglect that allowed vegetation to die or become overgrown. With various respites during periods of civic reform, these problems were to continue long after Olmsted's departure, eventually resulting in formation of a private Central Park Association in 1902 to supplement municipal maintenance and to resist efforts to appropriate park land.

The phenomenal success of Central Park from its opening day inspired similar efforts throughout America; Olmsted would have left a major design heritage, even if he had done nothing else in his career. At the same time, the size and quality of the park created still unresolved problems. In the light of his experience, the primary problems of urban parks emerge as those of design, maintenance, and evaluation of failure and success, problems which he was himself often hampered in solving by local conditions. Long after the original design had been adopted, Olmsted continued to study examples of the park's use and misuse, seeking new information for possible revision of his original design and for his later projects. His own sense of public responsibility as well as his talent for design provide a precedent and a model for today's urban planners.

Since Central Park's dedication outside influences have been continually trying to change Olmsted's original design concept. Short-sighted "land-grabbers" and well-meaning "improvers" have been equally at fault.

The outright appropriation of park land for zoos, theaters, or transport terminals is an obvious example of misuse. Just as injurious are a growing number of small concessions to "utility" which have eventually crowded out Olmsted's original purpose. Using the justification of increased maintenance problems, park administrators paved the pleasure drives. As traffic increased, they straightened curves, widened road sections, and removed trees for better visibility. Traffic lights and pedestrian crossings were added for safety. As the park became more accessible, traffic, fumes, and noise increased. Almost imperceptibly, through a series of minor decisions, a natural preserve became a traffic artery.

Moving with an impetus gained from the WPA era of the thirties, improvers organize to add something useful to the park because the land is there. They act on the assumption that if our parks have maintenance and police problems, private civic groups can solve them by adding some construction for active recreation—playgrounds, restaurants, and skating rinks, for example.

Most man-made structures, however, create their own environment; they can be built almost any place where there is available land. But the natural, uncluttered space that Olmsted strove to create can no longer be found anywhere else in the central city. The soothing effect of such open space is as important today as it was in the nineteenth century and its preservation increasingly important. Administration—preservation, maintenance, and policing—is of top priority for such parks. (The recent closing of Central Park roads to traffic on Sundays provides an example of how creative administration can help a park achieve its major purpose.) For designers and civic groups the real responsibility lies elsewhere. Olmsted's example provides a major challenge—not to imitate or restructure his designs but to provide new, urban space where little now exists.

DETAILS OF BIRKENHEAD PARK, ENGLAND

Designed by Sir Joseph Paxton. Olmsted's visit to this park in 1850 impressed him greatly: "Five minutes of admiration and a few more spent in studying the manner in which art had been employed to obtain from nature so much beauty and I was ready to admit that in democratic America there was nothing to be thought of as comparable with this People's Garden" — F.L.O.

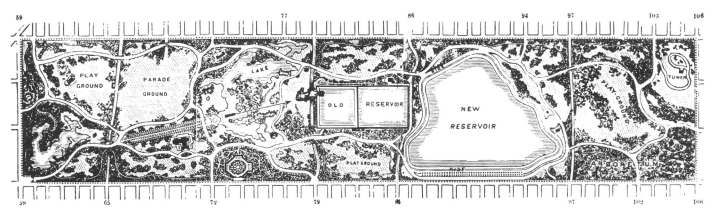

"GREENSWARD," THE ORIGINAL PLAN FOR CENTRAL PARK, 1858 (above)
MAP OF THE PARK AS IT APPEARED ca. 1870 (foldout, right)
Although there were numerous modifications of details, Olmsted and
Vaux's basic conception was carried out for the lower park
(below 85th Street); extension of the upper park to 110th Street
permitted them to develop that area, as they had the lower park,
in accordance with the natural topography. Sunken transverse roads
were included right from the beginning as a unique part of the
Olmsted-Vaux plan. In defense of the numerous grade divisions
Olmsted remarked that "to the visitor, carried by occasional defiles
from one field of landscape to another, . . . the extent of the park is
practically much greater than it would otherwise be"
[Olmsted Office Portfolio]

SKATING IN CENTRAL PARK, ca. 1860
Olmsted wished to provide for all forms of outdoor recreation: "There has been an attempt to segregate these areas and to develop them, each for its own function, so that . . . they may best provide all the forms of recreation which the community owes to its members"—F.L.O.
[Olmsted Office Portfolio]

UNDERPASS AND TRAFFIC ON TRANSVERSE ROAD, ca. 1861
Olmsted used underpasses and depressed roadways to preserve the harmony of nature: "The value of these grade separations lies not so much in the greater safety to pedestrians but chiefly in the . . . greater comfort for people who have come to the park for enjoyment"—F.L.O.
[Olmsted Office Portfolio]

[25]

CENTRAL PARK.

VIEW OF THE TERRACE AND FOUNTAIN, CENTRAL PARK, 1863 (above)
This area of the park particularly appealed to nineteenth-century taste.
Details of the Terrace are the work of Jacob Wrey Mould;
statues are by Emma Stebbins [Olmsted Office Portfolio]

OVERVIEW OF CENTRAL PARK, 1863 (left)
Explaining his conception of the use of the park land, Olmsted said that "it was
first of all, required that such parts of the site as were available and necessary to the
purpose should be assigned to the occupation of elements which would compose a
wood-side, screening incongruous objects without the park as much as possible from
the view of observers within it. Secondly, of the remaining ground, it was required
to assign as much as was available to the occupation of elements which would
compose tranquil, open, pastoral scenes. Thirdly, it was required to assign all of
the yet remaining ground to elements which would tend to form passages of
scenery contrasting in depth of obscurity and picturesque character of detail with the
softness and simplicity of the open landscape."
[New York Historical Society]

CENTRAL PARK IN THE 1960'S

Olmsted's predictions fulfilled: "No longer an open suburb, our ground [Central Park] will have around it a continuous high wall of brick, stone, and marble. The adjoining shore will be lined with commercial docks and warehouses; steamboat and ferry landings, railroad stations, hotels, theaters, factories, will be on all sides of it and above it; all of which our park must be made to fit" —F.L.O.

[Aero Service Division, Litton Industries]

TREE-MOVING MACHINE (left)
An example of the specialized equipment developed to recreate nature. In this case larger trees could be transplanted, and the lag between planting and finished appearance reduced
[Olmsted Office Portfolio]

PLAN OF PROSPECT PARK, BROOKLYN (right)
Olmsted's second major commission, and perhaps his best effort, echoes the concepts he developed in Central Park. Winding carriage roads and walkways, a lake and open fields in the lowlands, and wooded slopes and hilltops conform to the natural topography rather than clashing with it. "The Longmeadow" is an exceptionally well-designed green; the gentle curve and rolling surface cause a constantly expanding vista to be presented to the beholder. Olmsted had here, in contrast to Central Park, a better proportioned shape to work with and was able to use earth fill around the perimeter to screen views of the city
[Olmsted Office Portfolio]

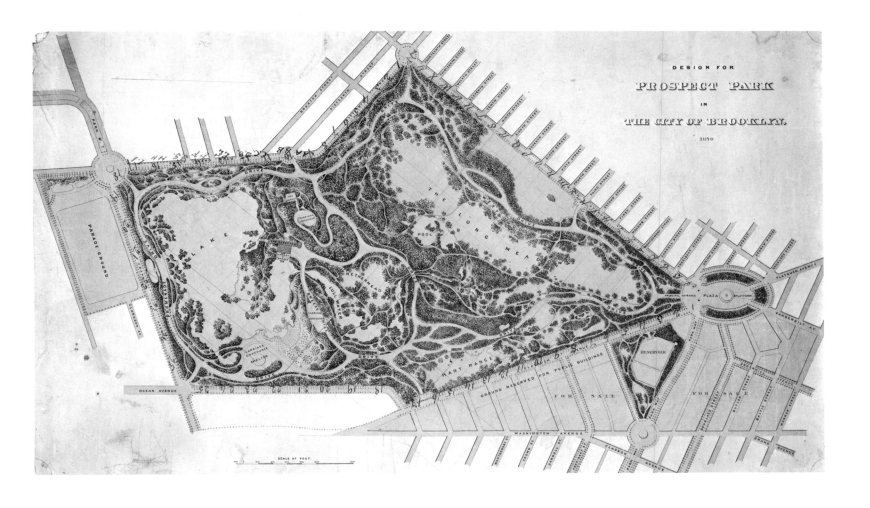

DESIGN FOR

PROSPECT PARK

IN

THE CITY OF BROOKLYN.

1870

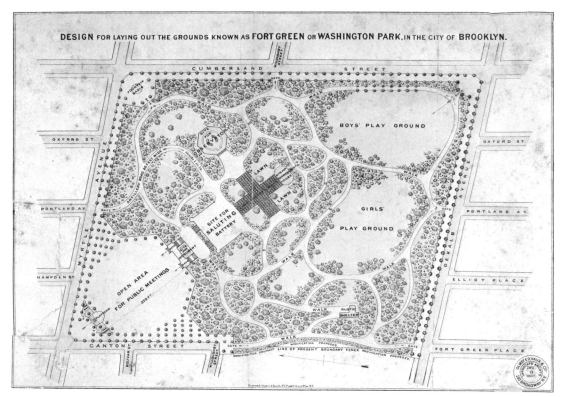

PLAN FOR FORT GREEN PARK, BROOKLYN
Also known as Washington Park. Over the years
Olmsted did a great deal of planning and park
work for the City (later Borough) of Brooklyn
[Olmsted Office Portfolio]

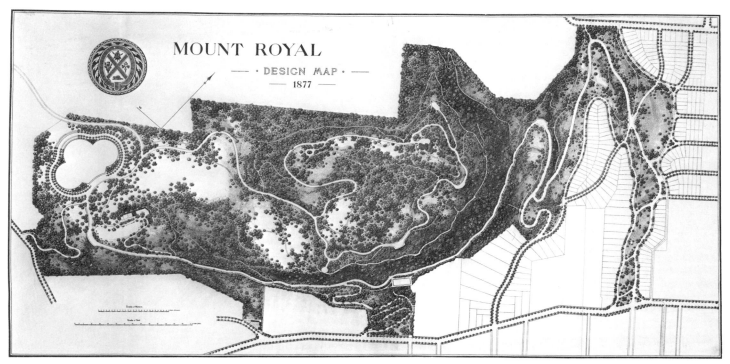

PLAN FOR MOUNT ROYAL, MONTREAL

*Mount Royal, a distinctive landmark overlooking the city,
offered a splendid opportunity for a park. Olmsted's
interest in Mount Royal began with a casual visit in 1873
and extended to ca. 1881. He not only provided the site
plan but also advised, via mail, on the construction
[Olmsted Office Portfolio]*

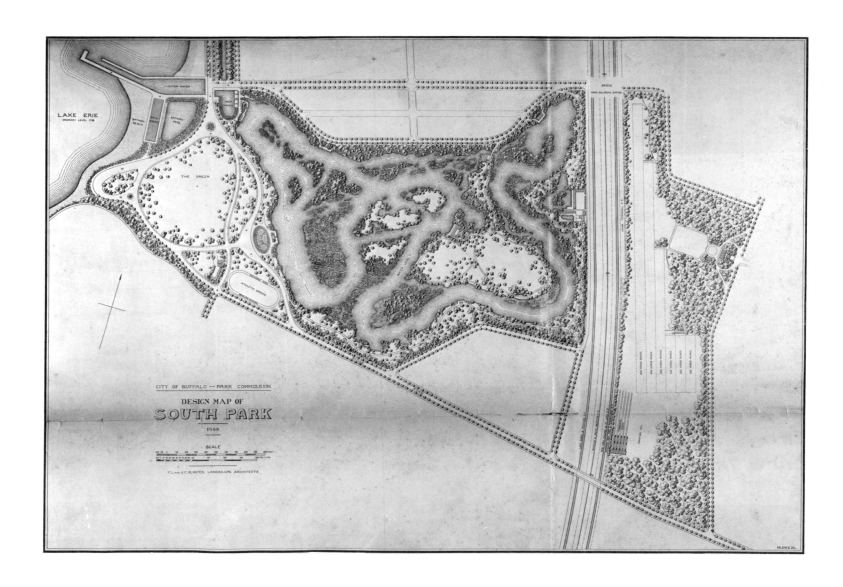

LAKE ERIE
ORDINARY LEVEL 7.8

THE GREEN

CITY OF BUFFALO — PARK COMMISSION.

DESIGN MAP OF

SOUTH PARK

1888

SCALE

F. L. AND J. C. OLMSTED, LANDSCAPE ARCHITECTS.

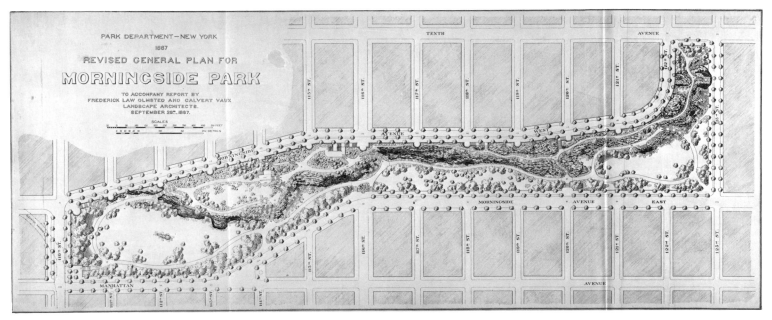

PLAN FOR MORNINGSIDE PARK, NEW YORK

*Olmsted's work on Manhattan Island included much
more than Central Park. Morningside Park was part
of his work as consulting landscape architect to the
New York Department of Public Parks*
[Olmsted Office Portfolio]

PLAN FOR SOUTH PARK, BUFFALO

*The Buffalo Park System was another with which
Olmsted was identified. In planning South Park, he had
Lake Erie as a plentiful source of water for a romantic
lagoon and island design*
[Olmsted Office Portfolio]

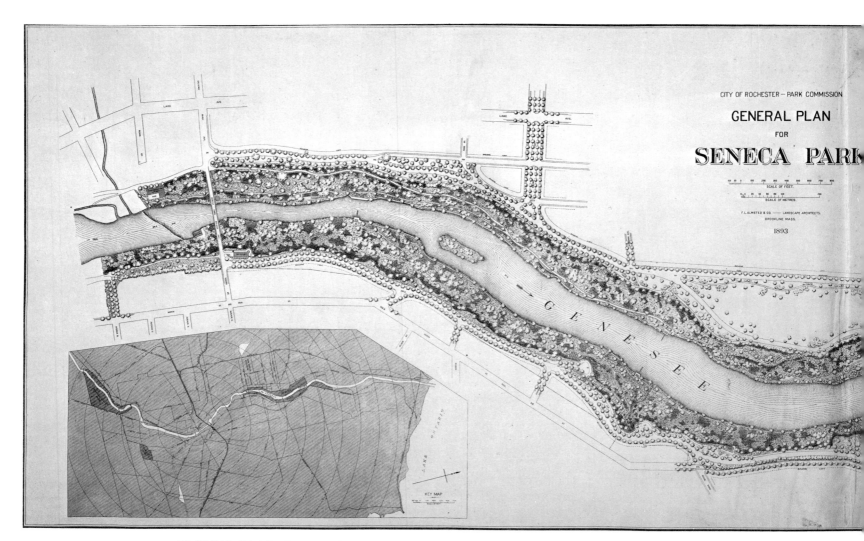

PLAN FOR SENECA PARK, ROCHESTER
Olmsted produced a spectacular linear park for Rochester.
His plan took best advantage of the natural topography
[Olmsted Office Portfolio]

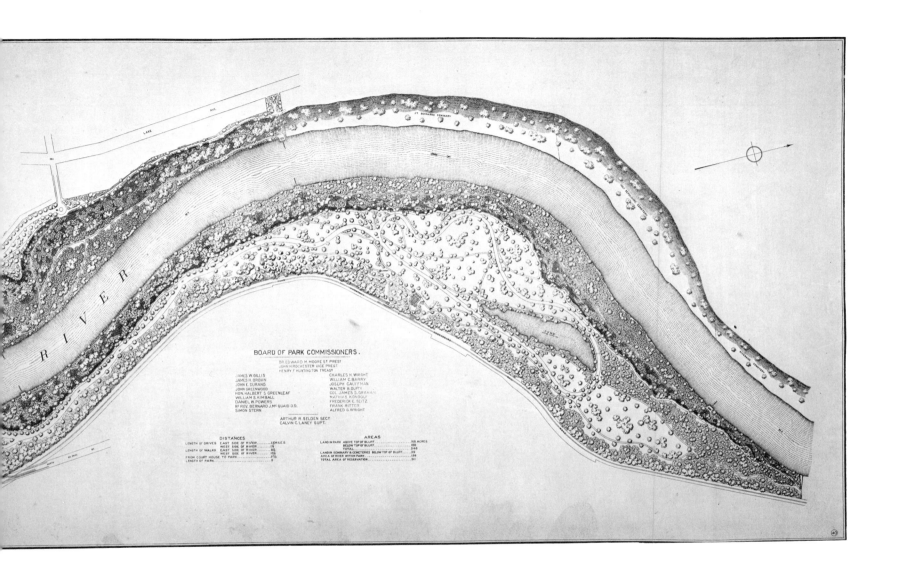

BOARD OF PARK COMMISSIONERS.

DR. EDWARD M. MOORE S? PRES?
JOHN H. ROCHESTER VICE PRES?
HENRY F. HUNTINGTON TREAS?

JAMES W. GILLIS
JAMES H. BROWN
JOHN E. DURAND
JOHN GREENWOOD
HON. HALBERT S. GREENLEAF
WILLIAM S. KIMBALL
DANIEL W. POWERS
R? REV. BERNARD J. M? QUAID D.D.
SIMON STERN

CHARLES H. WRIGHT
WILLIAM C. BARRY
JOSEPH CAUFFMAN
WALTER B. DUFFY
COL. JAMES S. GRAHAM
MATHIAS KONDOLF
FREDERICK C. SEITZ
FRANK RITTER
ALFRED G. WRIGHT

ARTHUR R. SELDEN SEC?
CALVIN C. LANEY SUPT.

DISTANCES		
LENGTH OF DRIVES	EAST SIDE OF RIVER	2¾ MILES
	WEST SIDE OF RIVER	1¼
LENGTH OF WALKS	EAST SIDE OF RIVER	8½
	WEST SIDE OF RIVER	10½
FROM COURT HOUSE TO PARK		2⅞
LENGTH OF PARK		3

AREAS	
LAND IN PARK ABOVE TOP OF BLUFF	168 ACRES
BELOW TOP OF BLUFF	180
TOTAL	348
LAND IN SEMINARY & CEMETERIES BELOW TOP OF BLUFF	39
AREA OF RIVER WITHIN PARK	126
TOTAL AREA OF RESERVATION	511

[37]

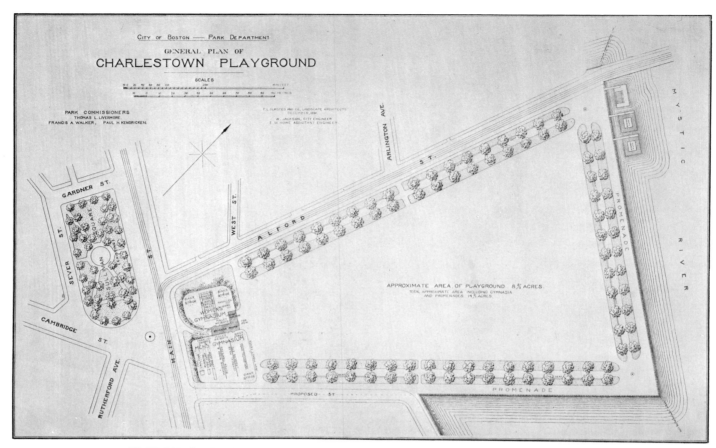

PLAN FOR CHARLESTOWN PLAYGROUND
*The nineteenth-century playground was simple
in comparison to the modern play-complex
[Olmsted Office Portfolio]*

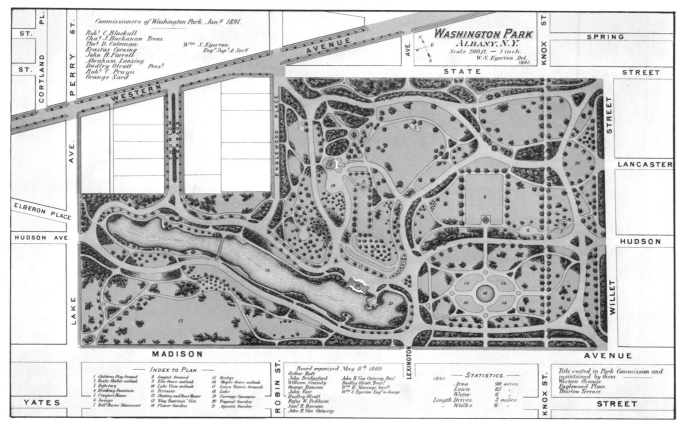

PLAN FOR WASHINGTON PARK, ALBANY

*Albany was another city which received the
special benefit of Olmsted's genius. As in most
of his other parks, the organically curving
road system is a hallmark
[Olmsted Office Portfolio]*

PLAN FOR JACKSON PARK, CHICAGO

The following is quoted from the note on the face of the plan: "The principal elements of the scenery of Jackson Park are (1) the Lake, (2) the Fields, and (3) the Lagoons. The broad view of Lake Michigan will be commanded from a Shore Drive and from a Concourse on Sunrise Bluff. . . . The Fields lying between the Lagoons and the Lake and between the Lagoons and the South-west Entrance present broad and quiet landscape of the simplest pastoral sort which will be pleasingly commanded from the adjacent drives and walks. It is designed to allow strolling and the playing of tennis and croquet upon these fields except when the turf needs resting. . . . The Lagoons, with their intricate and bushy shore lines, their beaches and bridges, and their almost complete seclusion, offer scenery in striking contrast to that of the Lake Shore and Fields. This scenery will be enjoyable from many points on the shore, but will be especially enjoyable when viewed from boats. . . . Contrasting with the rest of the park, the neighborhood of the vast building of the Columbian Field Museum is designed upon formal lines for the sake of architectural harmony."
[Olmsted Office Portfolio]

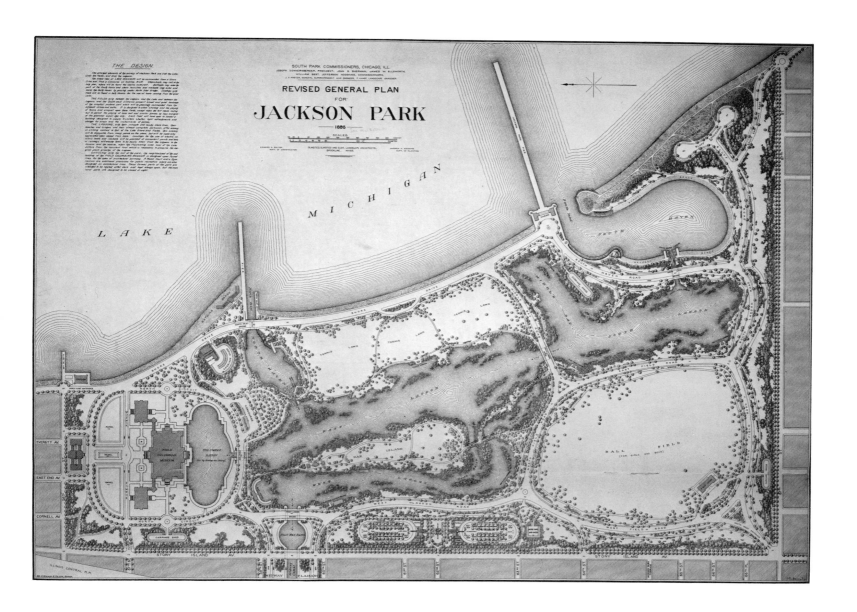

State and National Parks

With the materials nature provided, Olmsted spent much of his life recreating pastoral scenes in urban settings, but he was equally sensitive to the monumental beauty of America's virgin lands. Unlike the vistas and gentle slopes of Central Park, the fierce beauty of Niagara Falls or California's sequoia groves could not be created by human hands, but it could be preserved from human desecration. Experience in the eastern United States during the first half of the nineteenth century suggested that such preservation was mandatory.

By the time of the Civil War, rapid development had changed much of New England's landscape and almost completely removed her original timber. The lordly Hudson River Valley of New York's Romantic painters was soon to be cluttered with railroads and industry. Around major cities, the fields and marshes that had sheltered wildlife were being taken for commercial or residential land; industrial wastes polluted local streams where it had once been possible to scoop out fish by the barrelful; almost every wild tract had been exposed to lumbermen or mill owners who were little concerned with preserving virgin beauty.

Determined to avoid the mistakes of the East, Olmsted was one of the many nineteenth-century reformers who participated in the effort to create national parks throughout America—a many-sided battle which he himself saw as "a spontaneous movement . . . , which we conveniently refer to as the genius of civilization." Throughout his life he found himself involved in such activity; in this area his major achievement came early in his career when he helped draft legislation for establishment of the first state park in the United States.

Olmsted's involvement with national parks was an accidental by-product of his administrative problems as secretary of the United States Sanitary Commission.

Overwhelmed by the constant demands of official duties complicated by lack of adequate supplies, he resigned his position and in August 1863 assumed the superintendency of the Mariposa Mining Estate in California. His arrival coincided with a local movement to conserve some of the sequoia groves throughout the state; Olmsted plunged into this work. In the following months he helped prepare a national bill making the Yosemite Valley and the Mariposa Big Tree Groves into state reservations.

Subsequently appointed commissioner of these two reservations in September 1864, Olmsted supervised the preparation of an influential policy report to the California legislature defining the duties and responsibilities of administering this public land. This report is notable for its declaration that "the establishment by government of great public grounds for the free enjoyment of the people . . . is . . . justified and enforced as a political duty." Weighed against the contemporary exploitation of the land by the transcontinental railroads, Olmsted's foresight and ideals were in notable contrast to those of his age.

The legislation for Yosemite provided an early precedent for the national parks movement, which began officially with the establishment of Yellowstone National Park in 1879. In later years the firm of Olmsted and Vaux served as consultants for additional conservation projects. Their design for the preservation of Niagara Falls (1883) involved the elimination of buildings at the very edge of the falls and the provision for trees, walkways, and parks for the public.

Olmsted in fact felt that natural beauty, when it was possible to find it, was even more restful than man-made imitations of nature. His belief in the healing power of nature, expressed in articles and reports throughout his life, echoes the earlier sentiments of the New England Transcendentalists. It is particularly appropriate, therefore, that his firm should have been involved in preserving the splendor of a falls so often called "sublime" by ante-bellum writers. Based on a conviction that the wise preservation of such beauty is a key element of planning, Olmsted's conservation work reflects his belief in values greater than those of the moment and his basic insistence on looking ahead at least two generations.

MARIPOSA BIG TREE GROVE,
ca. 1863 (left)
YOSEMITE VALLEY, CALIFORNIA (right)
*Olmsted's imagination was caught by
the splendor of these giant trees and
of the unspoiled Yosemite Valley. He
labored to have these areas set aside as
state parks and helped form the
policies of the nascent conservation
movement: "The establishment by
government of great public grounds
for the free enjoyment of the people
. . . is . . . justified and enforced as a
political duty"—F.L.O.
[Ansel Adams Photograph]*

NIAGARA FALLS, ca. 1883
Olmsted and Vaux drew up general plans for the
preservation of this international treasure which had been
threatened with encroaching industry. In a pioneer example
of international cooperation, both Canadian and New
York State officials labored for a score of years to rescue
this sublime example of the New World's grandeur

Community Design

Immediately before and after the Civil War, metropolitan America began to develop its first commuter suburbs. Fast railroad service first enabled the city's wealthier families to flee the downtown and isolate themselves in clusters of turreted Victorian mansions surrounded by green fields. Later, the fields were to be filled with the newer houses of those who were only well-to-do and came by trolley. Even today the suburb, like the campus, provides an opportunity to create a unique sense of community.

Believing that "the mere proximity of dwellings which characterize all strictly urban neighborhoods is a prolific source of morbid conditions of the body and mind, manifesting themselves in nervous feebleness . . . and various functional derangements," Olmsted set out to create for the Riverside Development Association a community which represented "the best application of the art of civilization to which mankind has yet attained." With his partner, Calvert Vaux, Olmsted used careful planning to make the Chicago suburb a place to foster the "harmonious cooperation of men in a community and the intimate relationship and constant intercourse and interdependence between families."

Given practically free rein by the trustees of the organization chartered to develop the suburb, Olmsted and Vaux found themselves with a 1600-acre site admirably suited to the type of bedroom community being developed at the time. Located on a site six miles from Chicago, Riverside boasted both an efficient railroad link with the central city and attractive topography which sloped gently toward the Des Plaines River. To these inherent advantages Olmsted brought his own sensitivity to natural features.

Before Riverside, American suburban planners followed the practice of imposing a grid street pattern on whatever topography existed. Natural features such as hills and streams were treated as an inconvenience to be corrected or ignored. In Riverside, Olmsted established at least the foundation for more commodious community design.

His approach, as outlined in his firm's report to the trustees, is a classic for later developers of suburbs. The primary objective of the trustees, Olmsted insisted, should be the development of a general plan, the fault of most existing suburbs being that "no intelligent design has been pursued to secure . . . distinctly rural attractiveness." In the execution of Riverside, Olmsted reinforced this general plan by planting roadside trees in irregular clusters to give a spontaneous effect and exploit the beauty of massed foliage. To avoid the problem of ugly architecture, Olmsted also suggested in his report that "we can require that no house can be built within a certain number of feet of the highway, and we can insist that each householder shall maintain one or two living trees between his house and the highway line." Both suggestions were adopted.

In further efforts to create a rural atmosphere, Olmsted and Vaux stressed in their report the importance of unfenced parks and recreation grounds with the "character of informal village greens." Various such parks were to be scattered throughout the development, often with facilities for "croquets or ball grounds" or other "objects of general interest." Olmsted also suggested increased damming of the Des Plaines River for pleasure boating.

In designing their transportation network, Olmsted and Vaux again went far beyond the customs of their day. Interior roadways wound around interesting natural features; they focused on the river; they were often depressed to create a less disturbing effect on sight lines, and for the first time were deliberately curved—"the idea being," in Olmsted's words, "to suggest and imply leisure, contemplativeness, and happy tranquility."

Within the development, Olmsted suggested a separation of business and pleasure traffic. His most radical innovation, not actually adopted by Riverside,

[48]

VIEW OF CHICAGO,
NINETEENTH CENTURY
*Buildings come right to the
water's edge, and rivers seem
to be considered only as modes
of commercial transportation; the
natural water corridor has been
obliterated*

CHICAGO MILL DISTRICT, ca. 1883
*Olmsted sought to eliminate
such crowded, unhealthy conditions.
"The mere proximity of dwellings
which characterize all strictly
urban neighborhoods is a prolific
source of morbid conditions of the
body and mind, manifesting
themselves in nervous feebleness . . .
and various functional derangements"—F.L.O.*

was a six-mile pleasure parkway connecting the community with Chicago for the benefit of commuters who wished to ride their horses to and from work. (Later Olmsted projects in Boston and subsequent highway design after his death made full use of this concept.)

It is a great tribute to Olmsted that the first of his suburbs has managed to maintain its rural character for almost a century despite the increase in automobiles and urban growth. It is perhaps an even greater, if somewhat ambiguous, tribute that Riverside has been the complete or partial inspiration for subsequent developments throughout the country.

The arguments against such new subdivisions are familiar—space-consuming, single-income, they are most successful when designed for wealthy clientele. Planners of less wealthy subdivisions can often imitate only Olmsted's curving streets while ignoring his small parks and creative use of topography. The growing problems of urban sprawl have encouraged today's progressive designers to abandon free-standing developments in favor of cluster developments which combine a greater concentration of housing with preservation of natural features.

As a model for modern developments, Riverside suffers from many of the problems created by population growth and automobile technology. What is important today is its example. Attempts to preserve natural topography in modern design schemes are counterparts of Olmsted's treatment of the Des Plaines River. In days of look-alike housing, moreover, the responsibility of creating unique communities through site planning is even more evident. The concept of community-oriented design is, in fact, the basis for planning in America's hundred "new towns" now being initiated. Riverside marks the beginning of America's attempt to solve such problems in a responsible manner.

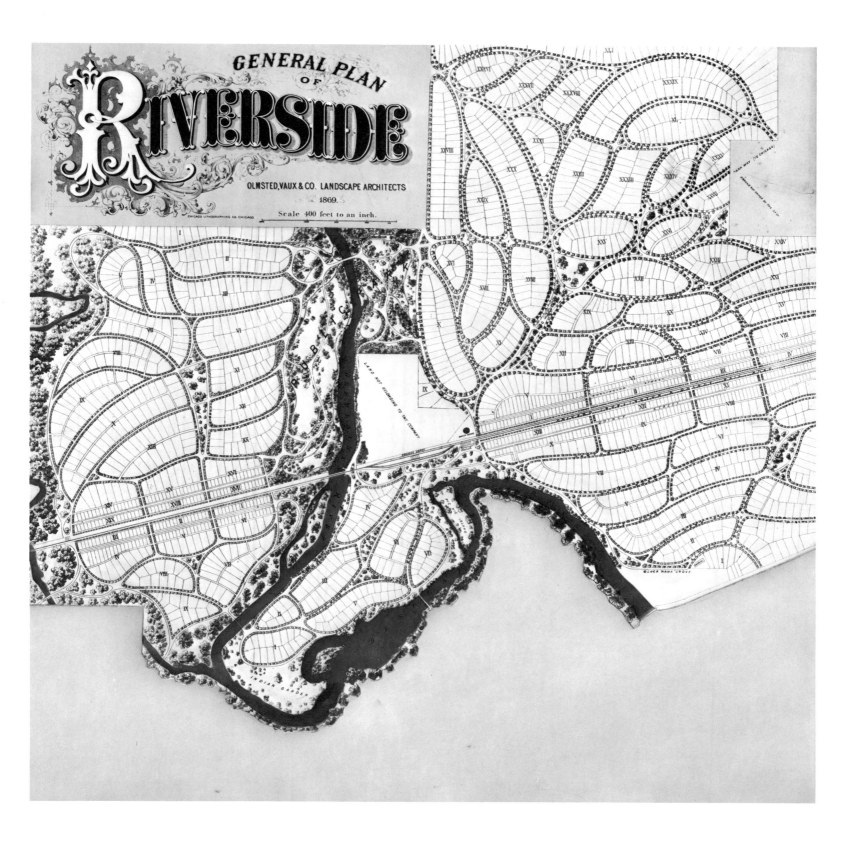

GENERAL PLAN
OF
RIVERSIDE

OLMSTED, VAUX & CO. LANDSCAPE ARCHITECTS
1869.

CHICAGO LITHOGRAPHING CO. CHICAGO

Scale 400 feet to an inch.

DETAILS OF RIVERSIDE
From a nineteenth-century promotional brochure. Olmsted saw the well-planned suburb as the place where one would find "the most attractive, the most refined, and the most soundly wholesome forms of domestic life, and the best application of the arts of civilization to which mankind has yet attained."

VIEWS OF RIVERSIDE TODAY
*Olmsted and Vaux preserved the land
along the river for a public common and,
rather than imposing a grid layout,
allowed their street plan to flow around
the landscape in harmony with the
meandering Des Plaines River.
Olmsted depressed the roadways to insure
that the expanses of green would be as
little broken visually as possible; he
specified a minimum setback and required
that each property have at least two trees
in front of the house
[William Tishler]*

RIVERSIDE TODAY

*Olmsted's park along the Des Plaines River still remains
as common land for the entire community. The dam
across the river increases the expanse of water
available for pleasure boating. The park provides an
area where residents of all ages can enjoy restful
natural surroundings. Depressed roadways
provide natural avenues to this open space
[William Tishler]*

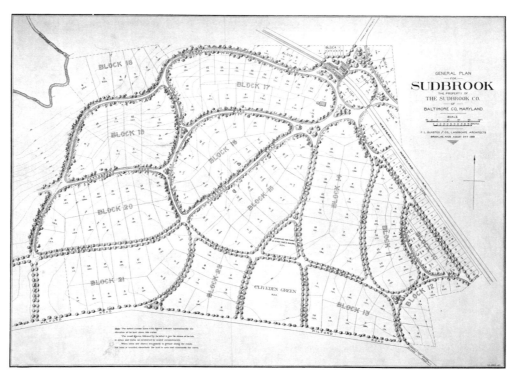

SUDBROOK SUBDIVISION, MARYLAND

*Here, as he had in Riverside, Olmsted sought
to reserve some common land and, within the
limits of existing roads, to make his street
layout conform to what nature had provided
[Olmsted Office Portfolio]*

Regional Planning

The ability to create patterns for regional growth requires two essential skills—understanding of the related problems of an extensive geographical area and talent for uniting solutions to many small problems in one overall plan. Olmsted possessed both skills in full measure. Although he never had the opportunity to apply them on a scale that is regional by modern definition, his comprehensive projects created precedents for later designers. In his plans for the development of Boston's Back Bay Fens area particularly, there are all the design and planning elements which later generations applied to larger geographical areas.

In practical terms, the Fens project was an operation to rid the city of a festering nuisance. Through Olmsted's genius, however, it also became a way of joining new and old sections of the city. By the 1870's, Boston had grown far beyond its original peninsula. Landfill operations had created the South End and Back Bay districts on both sides of the original neck that joined the city to the mainland; as its population grew the city had also expanded its political limits to include the mainland, suburban townships of Roxbury (1867) and Dorchester (1868). Draining these areas and forming the boundary between Boston and Brookline lay the Fens—a foul tidal swamp and creek left over from the days when all of Back Bay was a shallow body of salt water.

As a collector of sewage and swamp water, the Fens created a distinct health problem. (Residents of the immediate area were probably more concerned with its general stench.) Equally important was the problem of flood control. Emptying into Back Bay were two streams—Muddy River and Stony Brook. Together they drained several thousand acres in Roxbury, Dorchester, and the adjacent village of Brookline, and they both emptied into the tidal basin of the Charles River

[57]

through Back Bay. About once every ten years, when heavy run-off coincided with very full tides, these streams would back up, flooding the lowlands of Roxbury. Until the flooding and tidal fluctuations were eliminated, municipal development in the area would be stymied.

In 1875, the city created an independent, three-man Park Commission to develop a general park system for the expanded metropolis and to examine ways of dealing with the Back Bay drainage problem. This commission, in 1878, requested that Olmsted review the comparative drawings that had been submitted for the development of the new Back Bay park.

Rejecting the efforts of previous designers, Olmsted initiated a plan that would transform the Fens into a public park and at the same time solve the drainage problem. His first technical innovation was to control the amount of water in Back Bay by building tide gates where the Back Bay Fens flowed into the Charles River. Olmsted next proceeded to bury a huge sewage interceptor in the Boston side of the Fens basin. This conduit reduced health hazards and provided run-off for Stony Brook. At times of extremely heavy rains it was anticipated that the Fens parkland could serve as a temporary storage basin for run-off with no permanent damage to its vegetation. Filling in the land around this conduit, Olmsted finally created a stable, linear park which he used to link the older downtown area and the newer suburban sections of Boston.

Through geographical accident, exploited by careful planning, Olmsted was also able to use the Muddy River drainage area as a vital link in the "Emerald Necklace" which he stretched from Boston Common around the circumference of the city to Franklin Park in Dorchester. A tie to the Common already existed along the broad esplanade of Commonwealth Avenue; by judiciously mapping extensions of the Fens park system, Olmsted linked these elements with the Charles River, Muddy River, Jamaica Pond, the Arnold Arboretum, and Franklin Park. He himself helped plan many of the elements in this park system.

Within this system Olmsted was able to establish a hierarchy of uses later incorporated into many regional design schemes. His system created large- and medium-size parks for rural relaxation and picnicking, smaller landscaped areas with ponds for recreation, and linear parkland for pleasure drives, riding, and hiking. Sketches of circulation patterns, though not thoroughly carried out, suggest a separation of traffic into five distinct lanes: sidewalks and streets for access to houses, promenades for casual hikers and strollers, driveways for carriages, and saddle paths for horseback riders. Carefully planted with shade trees, such parkways could serve the triple purposes of delight, recreation, and circulation.

The effect of such comprehensive design was to create a strong precedent for later landscape architects. Charles Eliot, a Bostonian, had been trained under Olmsted; during the 1890's he followed Olmsted's lead by extending the metropolitan Boston park system to include the Blue Hills Reservation, the Middlesex Fells, and other open land immediately adjacent to the metropolitan area. When the Charles River was dammed in 1903, later planners followed Eliot's design for a complementary linear park along the riverbank on the site of its former tidal mudflats. In such work Eliot followed Olmsted's previous example by establishing several different types of park facilities to serve different public needs.

The original purpose of the Olmsted and Eliot plans was threefold: to make an engineering solution the occasion for creating a needed municipal open space; to link newly annexed communities to the historic municipal center; and to provide, as in Central Park, a variety of forms of recreation—pleasure driving, picnicking, and education at the Arboretum.

Over the years their park system has been broken up by parking lots, superhighways, and overpasses which have obliterated the linkages and destroyed the parks' recreational value in many areas. Even worse a good precedent has been replaced with a bad one. Today, instead of combining engineering and design as the occasion to turn potential eyesores into assets, engineers seem to design highways with no regard for aesthetic effect. Technology seems to have made recreation and transportation planning much less compatible than they were during Olmsted's life. Current plans call for even more highway construction over, under, and through his "Emerald Necklace."

[59]

The fate of the Back Bay points to a need for reassessing public development policy. Olmsted's original plan for the Fens called for a complementary balance of transportation, sanitation, and recreation. In modern times technology and population growth have enlarged the demands of transportation. Realistic plans for urban development must recognize the fact that major land arteries are no longer "improvements" for the residential city; they create barriers to local travel, require too much space, add too much noise, and pollute too much air. While it may be impossible to preserve every detail of Olmsted's plan for open space, it would seem that depressing and covering roadways would help to preserve some of Olmsted's balance between seemingly conflicting land uses.

THE METROPOLITAN BOSTON PARK SYSTEM, 1899
This map shows both the work of Olmsted and that
of his pupil and partner, Charles Eliot
[Olmsted Office Portfolio]

[61]

WORK ON THE FENS, BOSTON, ca. 1880
*Olmsted in attempting to solve the
problems of flood drainage and to create
linear recreation space within the
limits of existing topography directed
an extensive work force in the
filling and rearranging of every square
yard of the surface
[Olmsted Office Portfolio]*

THE RIVERWAY, BOSTON, ca. 1900
*Olmsted's ideals are achieved in the
tree-shaded walk and river
[Olmsted Office Portfolio]*

THE RIVERWAY, BOSTON, ca. 1900

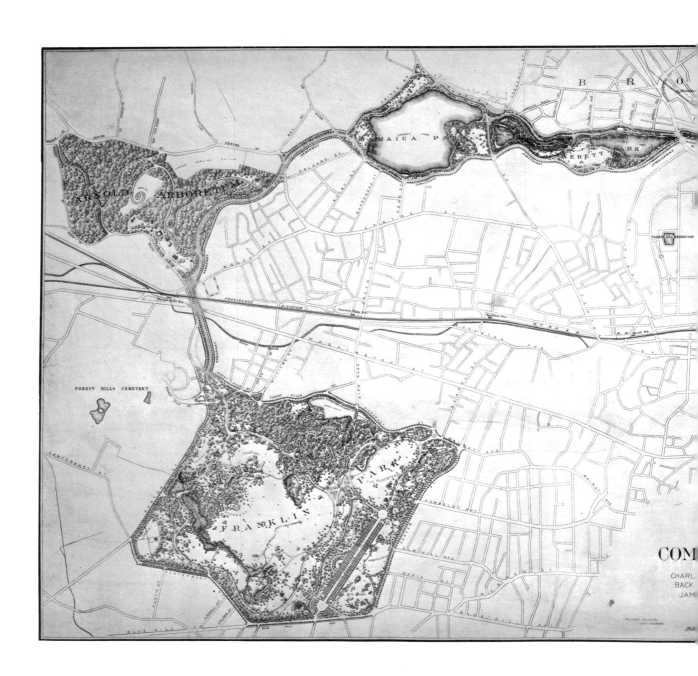

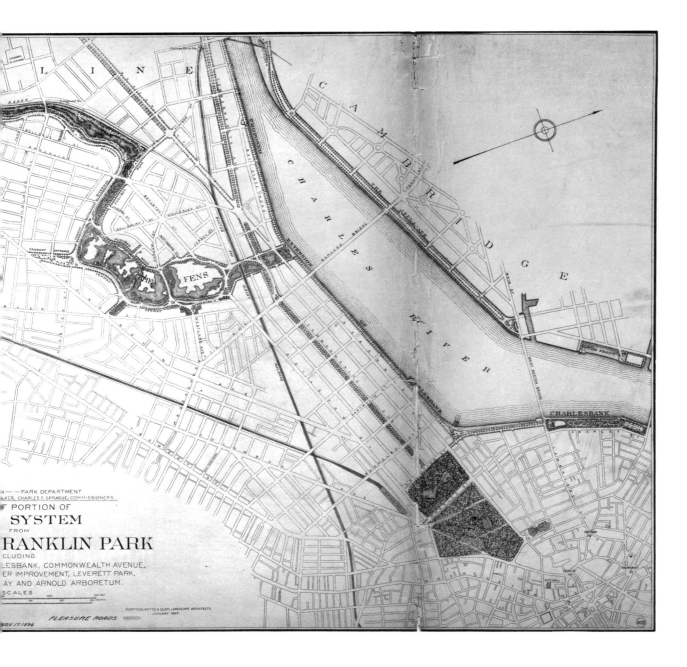

F PORTION OF

SYSTEM

FROM

RANKLIN PARK

CLUDING

LESBANK, COMMONWEALTH AVENUE,
ER IMPROVEMENT, LEVERETT PARK,
AY AND ARNOLD ARBORETUM.

SCALES

OLMSTED,OLMSTED & ELIOT, LANDSCAPE ARCHITECTS.
JANUARY 1894.

PLEASURE ROADS

NOV. 17. 1896

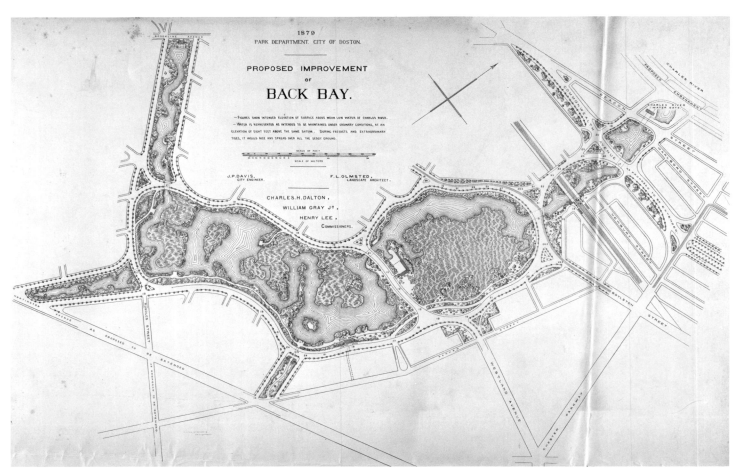

PLAN FOR BACK BAY, BOSTON
Olmsted combined a brackish tidal estuary (right)
with a fresh water stream (left), emptying
into the Charles River through an underground
channel, and produced what appears to be a
continuous river park
[Olmsted Office Portfolio]

[66]

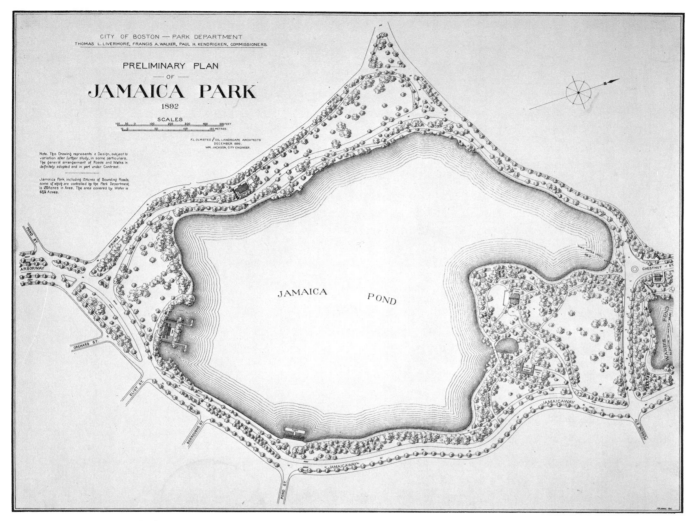

JAMAICA PARK AND POND, BOSTON
[Olmsted Office Portfolio]

GENERAL PLAN FOR FRANKLIN PARK, BOSTON, 1885

The following observation is quoted from the note on the face of the plan: "The entire property has been bought by the city because of its special advantages for one purpose. That purpose is to provide opportunity for a form of recreation to be obtained only through the influence of pleasing natural scenery upon the sensibilities of those quietly contemplating it. The larger part of the property, being the division designated 'The Country Park,' is proposed to be set apart with absolute exclusiveness for this purpose. That is to say, if this part of the park is to have value for any other purpose, it is designed that it shall occur but incidentally, and at no appreciable sacrifice of advantages for the quiet enjoyment of natural scenery. The division is a mile long and three-quarters of a mile wide. Natural scenery of much value for the purpose stated cannot be permanently secured on a tract of land of diversified surface, of these limits, with a great city growing about it, if the essential elements of such scenery are to be divided, belittled, diluted, or put out of countenance by artificial objects at all more than is necessary to its protection and to the reasonable convenience of those seeking the special benefits offered. The plan proposes, therefore, that nothing shall be built, nothing set up, nothing planted as a decorative feature; nothing for the gratification of curiosity, nothing for the advancement or popularization of science. These objects are provided for [elsewhere]. To sustain the designed character of the Country Park, the urban elegance generally desired in a small public or private pleasure ground is to be methodically guarded against." [Olmsted Office Portfolio]

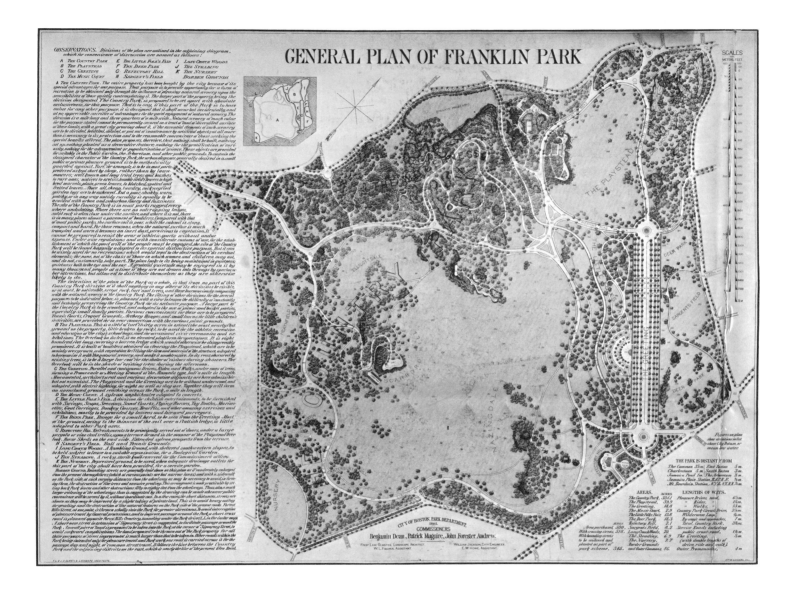

STREET FOR TRAFFIC — 40 FT. — 10 FT. — BUILDING LOTS. 200 FEET. — 20 FT. — PROMENADE 15 FT. — 20 FT. — DRIVE WAY. 60 FT. — 20 FT. — PARK-WAY 200 FEET WIDE FOR PLEASURE TRAVEL.

PROMENADE
15 FT. 10 FT. 40 FT. 10 FT.

STREET
FOR TRAFFIC.

BUILDING LOTS 200 FEET.

OLMSTED'S PRELIMINARY STUDY FOR
A BOSTON PARKWAY, 1881 (above)
THE ARBORWAY TODAY (below)
*Olmsted separated different
types of traffic (through and
local) and used the connecting
ways between different parts of
his park system as parks in
themselves and, indeed, as organic
parts of the whole "Emerald
Necklace." Today, precious little is
left of his tree-shaded parkways
[Olmsted Office Portfolio]*

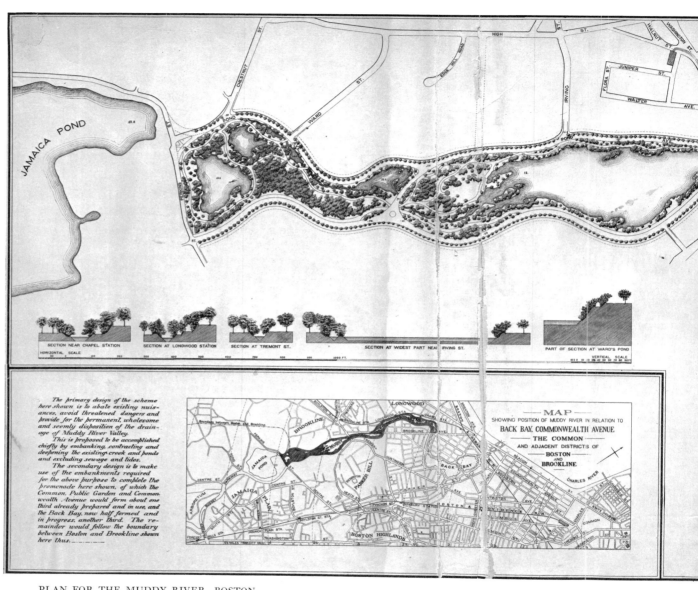

PLAN FOR THE MUDDY RIVER, BOSTON
Olmsted was at his best when following the natural contours of a river valley
[Olmsted Office Portfolio]

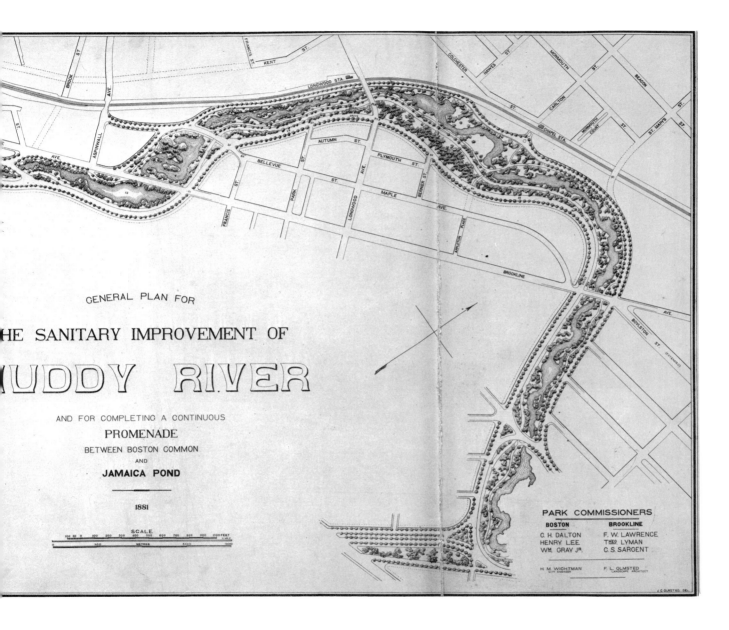

GENERAL PLAN FOR

HE SANITARY IMPROVEMENT OF

UDDY RIVER

AND FOR COMPLETING A CONTINUOUS

PROMENADE

BETWEEN BOSTON COMMON

AND

JAMAICA POND

1881

SCALE

PARK COMMISSIONERS

BOSTON   **BROOKLINE**

C. H. DALTON   F. W. LAWRENCE
HENRY LEE   THEO. LYMAN
WM. GRAY JR.   C. S. SARGENT

H. M. WIGHTMAN   F. L. OLMSTED
CITY ENGINEER   LANDSCAPE ARCHITECT

THE FENWAY TODAY (above)
*Insertion of a starkly modern elevated highway through
the center of Olmsted's romantic lagoons seems to
symbolize the fate of many of his best conceptions
[Bert Beaver]*

Campus Design

The necessity for planning campuses as large unified groups of buildings had existed in America since before the Revolution. Among the most famous examples were Jefferson's colonnaded University of Virginia (1819–1825) and Bullfinch's axial plan for Harvard Yard (1813). Olmsted's plan for Stanford University (1886) represented both a continuation of past traditions and their special adaptation to the characteristics of the California climate.

As the site consultant for Leland Stanford, Jr.'s new university, Olmsted followed the precedents of classical ante-bellum planning. The central entrance is clearly defined; arcades unify buildings with different functions, and important meeting areas are centrally located. In addition, Olmsted's final design greatly expanded the scale of most previous campus planning. Although it was not expected that Stanford would use all of its available land immediately, Olmsted's plan provided a clearly defined pattern for orderly expansion in harmony with his original design. The total site he projected for Stanford covers hundreds of acres, provides for adjacent faculty housing, and integrates academic and residential districts by axial road systems.

While elaborating on eastern precedents for his overall plan, however, Olmsted also adapted them to California's needs. In such warm, partially arid regions, heat and wind are the natural enemies of comfort. Olmsted's solution was to provide small, open spaces well protected from the weather. Shunning an open arrangement of buildings, he created a system of clustered courtyards and deep loggias. In adapting this plan from Mediterranean models, Olmsted was conscious of sacrificing "all that we have found agreeable" in the architecture of eastern colleges. Yet his connected, self-contained teaching units still reflect a similar vision of education as a series of individual disciplines joined by a common ideal.

The later history of Olmsted's site plan indicates some of the inherent problems of campus planning still with us today. Though a major portion of his proposal for the main college complex was carried out, in later years belief in his plan for an integrated campus had to yield to decisions based on changing academic needs and limited finances. Beyond the campus itself, his plans for related faculty residences were never completely fulfilled.

When the university opened in 1891 the classroom buildings surrounding the inner quadrangle were complete. The residence halls for men and women had also been finished and were situated in alignment with the outer quad buildings to the east and west. This fact indicates a very clear intention to carry out the original plan in full. Within a year, however, a neo-classical museum had been erected on a site west of the main drive and parallel to it in the area designated by Olmsted for residential development and schools. During the next two years, the construction of the outer quad buildings progressed as originally designed, but a separate chemistry building was situated in alignment with the museum, tentatively completing, as it were, one side of a Beaux-Arts composition bearing little relationship to the original concept.

Reconstruction after the earthquake of 1906 delayed further building for some years. The art gallery of 1917 conformed in plan and style to the original scheme for quadrangular extension of the central campus to the east and west, but the main library of 1919, built to the east of the inner quad, negated the entire concept since it blocked the planned interconnection. The total abandonment of the plan can be sensed in the location and form of the Hoover Institute of 1941 and in the modernistic physics lecture hall of 1957, built on axis with the library to the west of the inner quad.

During the post-war years of expansion a number of experts have been consulted. Architectural design has tended to perpetuate the red tile roofs of the original buildings and, budget permitting, has incorporated protected exterior circulation in the form of arcades. Part of the area to the south and west of the main quad was developed as a residential section according to the Olmsted plan. Since the Second World War this has been expanded and plans are now in hand for further development to the east.

Rather than the proposed linear form, the campus has grown in all directions around the central core. A major peripheral road with parking lots is being developed to contain the expanded core which will be closed ultimately to automobile traffic. Important pedestrian meeting places are being created in a formal manner and the connections between them, informally. Although Olmsted discouraged lawns in the west in favor of ground cover plants, the technology of irrigation systems and maintenance machinery now make grass surfaces easier and more economical to maintain; consequently, the space between buildings now frequently contains grass areas.

In general, the efforts of the university in conjunction with the skills of local professionals promise the development of a campus environment, different from that envisaged by Olmsted, but, nonetheless, retaining the sense of unostentatious scholarly dignity toward which the nineteenth-century designer aspired.

The chaos beginning to surround many rapidly-growing major universities suggests the wisdom of taking a new look at Olmsted's approach to Stanford. Although he himself recognized that every master plan must be reviewed constantly to meet changing conditions, such plans are a necessity in providing beauty and coherent development in the midst of inevitable change.

A STANFORD UNIVERSITY QUADRANGLE TODAY (above)
[Stanford University]

RENDERING OF STANFORD UNIVERSITY, ca. 1886 (foldout right)
[Olmsted Office Portfolio]

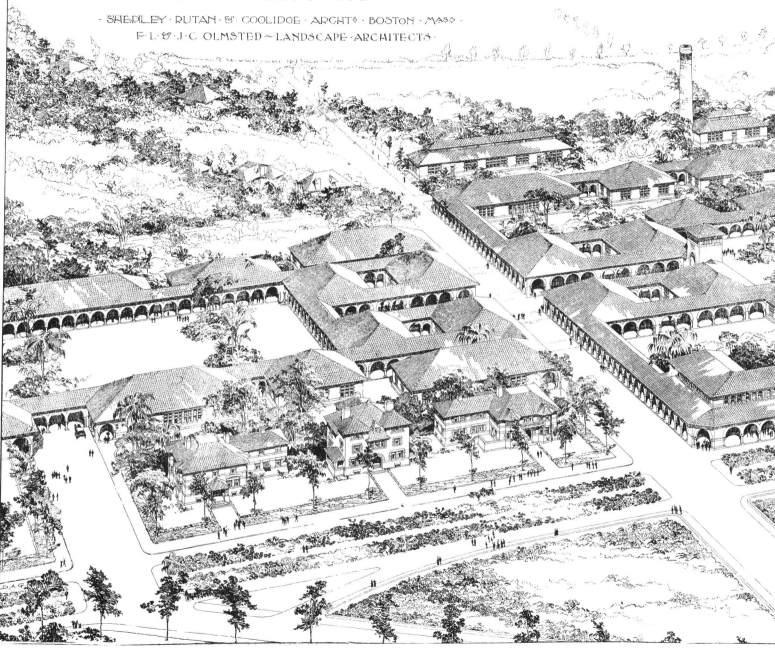

THE
LELAND · STANFORD · JR · UNIVERSITY ·
· PALO · ALTO · CAL ·
· SHEPLEY · RUTAN · & · COOLIDGE · ARCHTS · BOSTON · MASS ·
F · L · & · J · C · OLMSTED ~ LANDSCAPE · ARCHITECTS ·

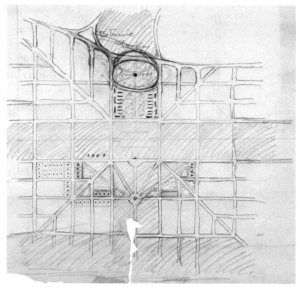

THE EVOLUTION OF A MASTER PLAN
Phase I (above), Phase II (below)
Olmsted's rough sketches reflect the careful thought involved in the development of Stanford's site plan; as the plan develops, the entire orientation of the campus is rotated about the central quadrangle. Olmsted continually tried various solutions to his problems as he allowed the design to grow in accordance with its own élan. Never did he try to impose preconceived solutions on what was always a new problem
[Olmsted Office Portfolio]

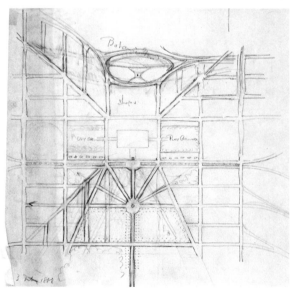

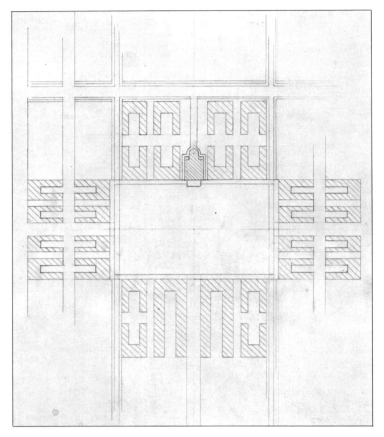

PRELIMINARY SKETCH FOR STANFORD'S
CENTRAL QUADRANGLE (left)
*Although the central quad and chapel
are evident, provision for axial
expansion is not yet apparent*
[Olmsted Office Portfolio]

FINAL SITE PLAN FOR THE
CENTRAL PREMISES OF STANFORD, (right)
*Here the notion of axial,
quadrangular expansion is fully
developed. Olmsted's plan, although
not cast in the usual neo-classical mold,
still provides an enclosed scholarly
environment*
[Olmsted Office Portfolio]

THE · LELAND · STANFORD · JUNIOR · UNIVERSITY ·
PLAN · OF · CENTRAL · PREMISES ~ 1888 ·

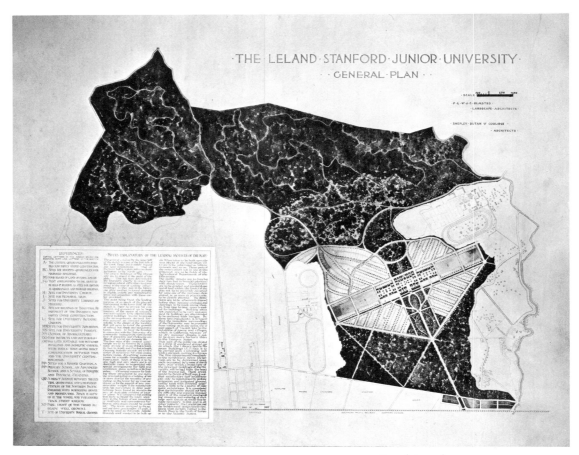

FINAL SITE PLAN FOR THE ENTIRE STANFORD ESTATE, ca. 1890 (above)
[*Olmsted Office Portfolio*]

STANFORD UNIVERSITY AND SURROUNDING AREA TODAY (right)
*South is to the top of the photograph. Chemistry building and
art museum (ca. 1890) are to the lower right of oval approach drive.
Library (1919) and Hoover Institute (1947) are to the left of central
quadrangle; the science complex (begun 1957) is to immediate right
[Sunderland Aerial Photographs]*

[82]

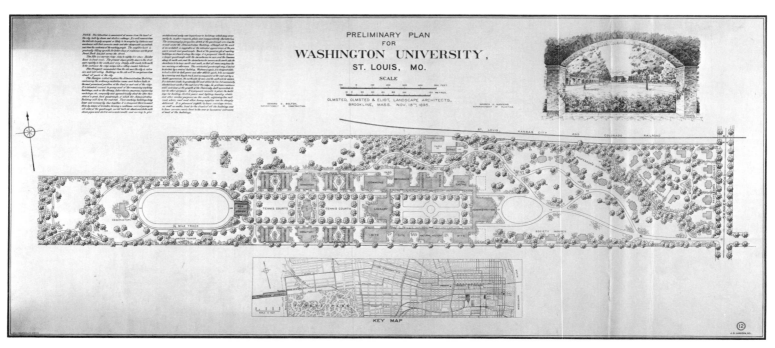

PLAN FOR WASHINGTON UNIVERSITY, ST. LOUIS
One of the numerous campus projects on which
Olmsted's office worked. These presented a splendid
opportunity for design of a self-enclosed, self-relating
community in which every aspect could be directed
toward a single effect
[Olmsted Office Portfolio]

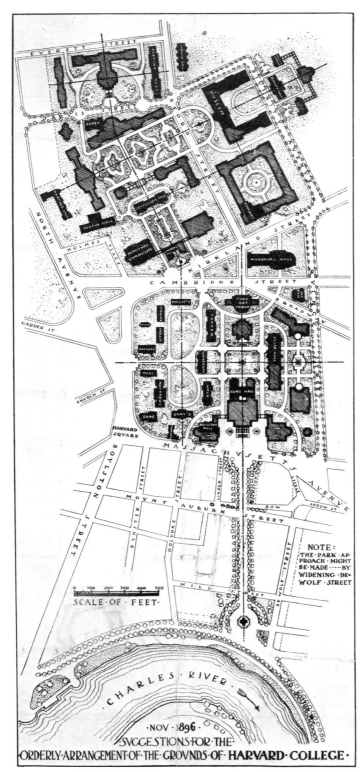

SUGGESTIONS FOR IMPROVEMENT OF
THE HARVARD CAMPUS, CAMBRIDGE,
MASSACHUSETTS, ca. 1886
*Olmsted's friendship with Charles
Eliot Norton led to a series of
suggestions (1868 ff.) regarding
Harvard property. One of his
concerns was to provide a direct
campus-oriented connection
between the Yard and the Charles
River. This plan, prepared for
Harvard by Olmsted's office after
his retirement and never carried out,
reflects the influence of his
discussions with Norton and with
co-workers.
This plan was actually prepared
by F. L. Olmsted, Jr.*
[Olmsted Office Portfolio]

Estate Design

By the last quarter of the nineteenth century the fabled rise of the great American fortunes was well under way. Rogues, bankers, merchants, publishers, inventors, and thieves were among those whose families felt the Midas Touch of the industrial revolution. Such men wanted estates to confirm their status and landscape architects to plan the estates. Commissions from the very wealthy were to dominate professional work from the Gilded Age through the Roaring Twenties.

Men of that era were more open in their display of wealth than are the well-to-do of our own day. Their country homes filled a public function by emphasizing the power and agricultural interests of America's new "aristocracy," and the size was at least one measure of success. The well-publicized estates of the last century were huge. George Washington Vanderbilt, aged thirty-three, could stand on the porch of his French château, near New Raleigh, North Carolina, and gaze toward the Blue Ridge Mountains just on the horizon. All the land in between and as far as the eye could see in any direction belonged to him. Such vast tracts of land under single management provided landscape architects with an opportunity for private conservation often unavailable in public commissions.

Olmsted's career was drawing to a close as the era of the great estates began. Although his preferences lay elsewhere, his office found itself increasingly involved in estate design. Among many such projects, Biltmore, North Carolina (1893) represents one of Olmsted's best personal efforts. Perhaps one reason for its success was the personal character of the owner. George Washington Vanderbilt, grandson of the Commodore, son of William, was an ardent conservationist. His interest in experimental farming, forestry, and horticulture led to the assembling of a vast tract of virgin forest, scrub growth, and fertile farmland among the hills of North Carolina. Employed to supervise the improvement and initial management of this land, Olmsted treated the private estate as a semi-public preserve—as land under private management being held for the future benefit of the public.

Biltmore's main building and its gardens suggest that estate design involved a somewhat different treatment of land than did the creation of public parks. The eclectic mansion designed by Richard Hunt became the focus of a neo-classical landscape design, one which dominated natural topography. Elsewhere on the estate Olmsted helped develop a 4,000-acre tree farm and arboretum to promote the most advanced methods of conservation. The road system he designed for Biltmore created handsome vistas, solving the problem of topography by making it "a matter of curving pleasure drives and hidden approaches." It suggests qualities of later public, scenic drives (such as Virginia's Blue Ridge Parkway) that wind through rural America.

In dedicating his work at Biltmore to results that might not be achieved for generations, Olmsted foresaw that such private work might still realize public good. His sophisticated approach is particularly relevant today. Many owners of large estates are deeding them to the public in their wills. Tanglewood, an estate which Olmsted's firm had designed in 1883, in Lenox, Massachusetts, for example, now houses the summer concerts of the Boston Symphony Orchestra.

The history of Biltmore also justifies Olmsted's foresight. Today, 12,000 acres of the original 100,000 in the estate, including the mansion, have become a school of forestry and the core of North Carolina's Pisquah State Forest. In this case, as in many later efforts of Olmsted's successors, private estate work was only the precursor of a long-range effort for public conservation.

CHÂTEAU AT BILTMORE,
ca. 1900
*The domineering structure
forced a neo-classical
treatment of the grounds
around it; elsewhere on the
property Olmsted followed
his usual less-formal style*
[Olmsted Office Portfolio]

WINDING ROADWAY IN THE
BILTMORE ESTATE, ca. 1893
*Olmsted here, as in all his
work, followed the dictates
of natural topography*
[Olmsted Office Portfolio]

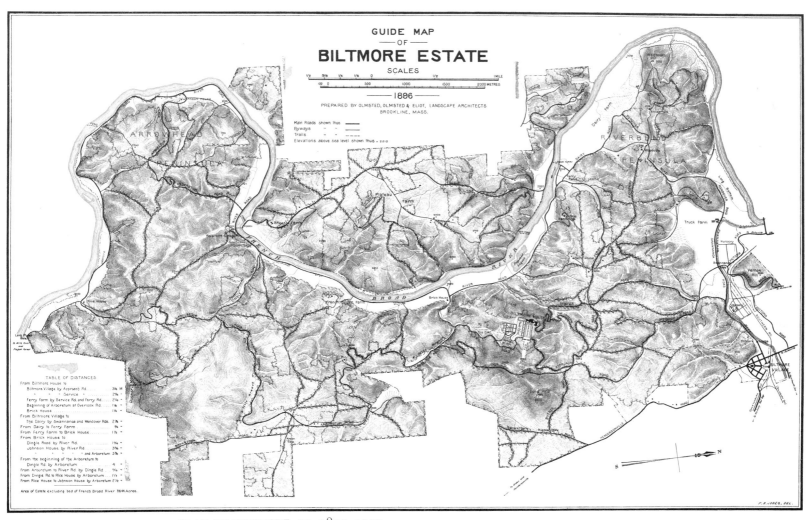

PLAN OF BILTMORE, ca. 1890–1900

Olmsted found Biltmore particularly satisfying because

he had unhampered control over an immense 100,000-acre tract of land

which he felt served as a "semi-public preserve"

[Olmsted Office Portfolio]

[89]

Urban Design

The original source of the great international expositions, now called World's Fairs, came from the industrial revolution. Eager to show off their wares and interested in experimenting with new possibilities in architecture, nations throughout Europe sponsored five great conclaves from 1851 to 1889; main features of these shows were demonstrations of the most advanced industrial products housed in huge halls of glass and iron made possible by advancing technology in the casting of metal. In 1890 the merchants of Chicago determined to make a name for their city by sponsoring a similar exposition in honor of the four-hundredth anniversary of America's discovery.

In concept and execution, the Columbian Exposition was a major landmark in American urban design. Architects, businessmen, artists, and landscape architects worked closely together in a commission under the chairmanship of Daniel Burnham. The physical result of this close collaboration was a resplendent white city, unified in architecture and transportation patterns, stretching for acres over the former sand flats of Jackson Park on the edge of Lake Michigan and along the midway to the west.

Much of the successful design of the Exposition was the result of Olmsted's personal effort. Commissioned as site designer, he gave careful consideration to possible locations, turning in a voluminous report weighing the merits of the five most likely possibilities. The eventual site was not his first choice; he had preferred a location with the double advantages of natural vegetation and immediate proximity to the center of the city. When local railroads could not be persuaded to lay the necessary extra tracks, however, Olmsted took as second choice a treeless marsh at the edge of the lake which had been reserved as parkland twenty years

[90]

previously. The site itself featured a shallow lagoon formed by the silting of a creek draining into the lake. By dredging the surrounding marshes and filling the resulting sludge behind strong vertical retaining walls Olmsted created terraces for buildings, deepened the lagoon, and formed the great central basin for the Exposition's Court of Honor. From this basic, man-made topography rose the monumental complex that did much to capture the visitor's imagination and shape subsequent American taste.

Olmsted's next major contribution to the success of the Exposition was his study for its circulation patterns. Although the eventual site plan did not follow all his recommendations, his hand is evident in the vistas and pedestrian links between important buildings and in the use of a variety of public spaces to create visual order. In the final site plan the entire Exposition was linked to a major transport system, and the railroad station became an important focal point of design. Borders of the site were unified, moreover, by a circumferential trolley system; the treatment of the interior as a series of superblocks with interior pedestrian corridors allowed for free circulation of vehicles and strollers. There were even a moving sidewalk and boat transportation in the lagoon and on the lake.

Architecturally, the Exposition was a great popular success. The decision of the Exposition committee to design all major buildings in a uniform neo-classical Beaux-Arts style resulted in an imposing collection of huge plaster façades displayed to their best advantage by the public spaces Olmsted had insisted it was necessary to provide. Wondering visitors came to admire and returned home to imitate, convinced that their cities could capture some of the Exposition's grandeur. Such cities as Cleveland, Chicago, and San Francisco began the first general effort to impose a sense of style and order on the chaotic street patterns and eclectic façades of their industrial cities. The idea of planning as a major collaborative effort involving designers, planners, and businessmen gained its first general acceptance.

Many later designers feel strongly that the Exposition was an aesthetic disaster because it turned public taste to the admiration of superficial façades. For this

Olmsted was not responsible, nor should he take the blame for the less obvious misinterpretations of his site plans by later planners. In designing settings for what was essentially a series of exhibition halls, Olmsted created his spaces in the full knowledge that there would be a public to fill them. His comprehensive approach to site planning, moreover, was essentially a characteristic of a disciplined approach to total urban design. When later applied in fragmentary fashion to isolated portions of a city, such as government centers, the same approach tended to produce dull and empty plazas. Few planners realized how much life the noise, movement, and activity of the Exposition visitors had added to dead classical façades. This is a lesson that designers of our modern plazas are again learning from experience.

Olmsted's last major contribution to American design illustrates both the scope of his genius and the paradox of its frustration in a world of less-observant designers. He considered each site as a problem in itself to be solved according to the best ideals of design and social function. In so doing, he helped create major land forms used for the next hundred years in creating livable spaces for America. But, when subsequent designers forgot his innovation and attempted to imitate only his style, they overlooked an essential element of the genius that had enabled him to reshape America.

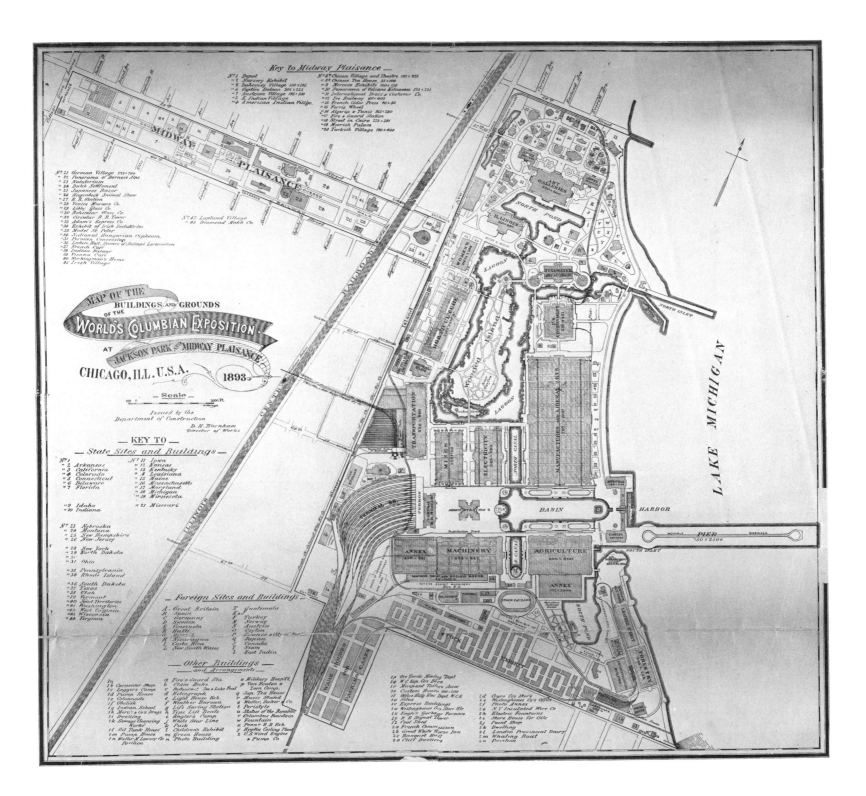

Key to Midway Plaisance

Nº 1 Depot
" 2 Nursery Exhibit
" 5 Dahomey Village 150 x 195
" 6 Captive Baloon 205 x 225
" 7 Austrian Village 185 x 330
" 3 E. Indian Village
" 4 American Indian Village

Nº 8 Chinese Village and Theatre 191 x 225
" 8 Chinese Tea House 55 x 100
" 9 Morocco Exhibits 150 x 150
" 9 Panorama of Volcano Kilauea 135 x 225
" 11 International Dress & Costume Co.
" 12 Ice Railway 40 x 400
" 15 French Cider Press 40 x 50
" 15 Ferris Wheel
" 16 Algeria & Tunis 165 x 280
" 17 Fire & Guard Station
" 18 Street in Cairo 225 x 291
" 19 Moorish Palace
" 20 Turkish Village 190 x 450

Nº 21 German Village 225 x 700
" 22 Panorama of Bernese Alps
" 23 Natatorium
" 24 Dutch Settlement
" 25 Japanese Bazar
" 26 Hagenbeck Animal Show
" 27 R. R. Station
" 28 Venice Murano Co.
" 29 Libby Glass Co.
" 30 Bohemian Glass Co.
" 32 Circular R. R. Tower
" 33 Adam's Express Co.
" 34 Exhibit of Irish Industries
" 35 Model St. Peter
" 14 National Hungarian Orpheum
" 31 Persian Concession
" 36 Lecture Hall, Science of Animal Locomotion
" 37 French Café
" 38 Indian Bazaar
" 39 Vienna Café
" 40 Workingman's Home
" 41 Irish Village

Nº 42 Lapland Village
" 43 Diamond Match Co.

MAP OF THE
BUILDINGS AND GROUNDS
OF THE
WORLD'S COLUMBIAN EXPOSITION
AT
JACKSON PARK AND MIDWAY PLAISANCE
CHICAGO, ILL. U.S.A.   1893

Scale
100   0   1000 Ft.

Issued by the
Department of Construction
D. H. Burnham
Director of Works

KEY TO
State Sites and Buildings

Nº 1
" 2 Arkansas
" 3 California
" 4 Colorado
" 5 Connecticut
" 6 Delaware
" 7 Florida

" 9 Idaho
" 10 Indiana

Nº 11 Iowa
" 12 Kansas
" 13 Kentucky
" 4 Louisiana
" 15 Maine
" 16 Massachusetts
" 17 Maryland
" 18 Michigan
" 19 Minnesota

" 21 Missouri

Nº 23 Nebraska
" 24 Montana
" 25 New Hampshire
" 26 New Jersey

" 28 New York
" 29 North Dakota
" 30
" 31 Ohio

" 32 Pennsylvania
" 34 Rhode Island

" 36 South Dakota
" 37 Texas
" 38 Utah
" 39 Vermont
" 40 Joint Territories
" 41 Washington
" 42 West Virginia
" 43 Wisconsin
" 44 Virginia

Foreign Sites and Buildings

A. Great Britain
B. Spain
C. Germany
D. Sweden
E. Venezuela
F. Haiti
G. Brazil
H. Nicaragua
I. Costa Rica
L. New South Wales

T. Guatemala
K.
M. Turkey
N. Norway
O. Austria
P. Ceylon
Q. Siam & City of Paris
R. Japan
S. Canada
X. Siam
Z. East India

Other Buildings
and Arrangements

1a
1b Carpenter Shop
1c Loggers Camp
1d Pump House
1e Colonnade
1f Obelisk
1g Indian School
1h Marc's Ore Drugs
1i Dwelling
1k Sewage Cleaning
   Works
1l Oil Tank House
1m Pump House
1n Walter A. Lowry Co.
   Pavilion

a Fire & Guard Sta.
b Clam Bake
c Reharous Sea's Lake Food
d Heliograph
e Light House Exh.
f Weather Bureau
g Life Saving Station
h Type Life Boats
i Angler's Camp
j White Star Line
k Puck
l Children's Exhibit
m Green House
n Photo Building

o Military Hospitl.
p Van Houten &
   Zoon Comp.
q Jap. Tea House
r Music Stand
s Waller, Baker & Co.
t Peristyle
u Statue of the Republic
v Columbian Fountain
w Fountain
x Hygeia Cooling Plant
y U.S. Wind Engine
  & Pump Co.

1p Ore Yards Mining Dept.
1q W. C. Exp. Co's Bldgs.
1r Merchant Tailors Assoc.
1s Custom House 100 x 200
1t Office Bldg Elec Dept. W.C.E.
1u Silos
1v Express Buildings
1w Westinghouse Co's Show Bldg
1x Engle's Garbage Furnace
1y R. R. Signal Tower
1z Coal Shed
2a French Commission
2b Great White Horse Inn
2c Banquet Hall
2o Cliff Dwelling

2d Crane Co's Store
2e Westinghouse Co's Office
2f Photo Annex
2g N. Y. Insulated Wire Co
2h Electric Fountains
2i Store House for Oils
2j Paint Shop
2k Dwelling
2l London Provincial Dairy
2m Whaling Boat
2n Pavilion

LAKE MICHIGAN

NORTH POND

NORTH INLET

PIER 50 x 2500
SOUTH INLET

BASIN   HARBOR

SOUTH POND

ADMINISTRATION B.

ANNEX MACHINERY   AGRICULTURE 500 x 800
ANNEX 550 x 550

TRANSPORTATION

MANUFACTURES AND LIBERAL ARTS

MINES   ELECTRICITY

HORTICULTURE

Wooded Island

LAGOON

FISHERIES

ILLINOIS

ART GALLERIES 320 x 500

WOMEN'S

U.S. GOVERNMENT

TERMINAL R.R.

MIDWAY PLAISANCE

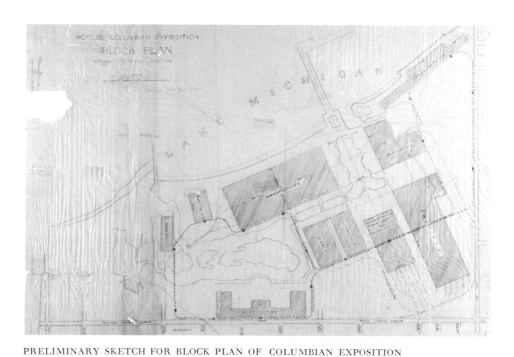

PRELIMINARY SKETCH FOR BLOCK PLAN OF COLUMBIAN EXPOSITION

An adumbration of the modern "superblock" concept, particularly noteworthy is the provision for perimeter circulation. Speaking of Olmsted's contribution to the Exposition, D. H. Burnham said: "Each of you knows the name and genius of him who stands first in the heart and confidence of American artists, the creator of your own parks and many other city parks. He it is who has been our best adviser and common mentor. In the highest sense he is the planner of the Exposition—Frederick Law Olmsted. No word of his has fallen to the ground among us since first he joined us some thirty months ago. An artist, he paints with lakes and wooded slopes; with lawns and banks and forest-covered hills; with mountainsides and ocean views. He should stand where I do tonight, not for his deeds of later years alone, but for what his brain has wrought and his pen has taught for half a century."
[Olmsted Office Portfolio]

VIEW OF THE BASIN AND THE MAIN HALL COLUMBIAN EXPOSITION
Olmsted provided large open spaces as a forum for the crowds
[The Bettmann Archive]

VIEW OF THE MAIN COURT AND BASIN OF THE EXPOSITION LOOKING EAST

[The Bettmann Archive]

VIEW OF THE MAIN COURT AND BASIN LOOKING WEST

[The Bettmann Archive]

OVERVIEW OF THE COLUMBIAN EXPOSITION

*In the man-made lagoon the wooded island echoes the romantic treatment,
nearly forty years earlier, of Central Park*

America's Designer

By the end of his lifetime Olmsted's projects covered the continent from New York to San Francisco and from Montreal to New Orleans. The success of Central Park showed that for the first time America had found a planning talent sufficient to the task of anticipating national needs. Later years proved Olmsted able to train others in his skills.

At a time when even schools of architecture were almost nonexistent in America, Olmsted's office educated most of the later leaders in landscape architecture—among them Henry Codman, Charles Eliot, Arthur A. Shurcliff, and Frederick Law Olmsted, Jr. These men later trained their own office staffs using Olmsted's techniques. Today there are over thirty schools of landscape architecture in America. City planning (developed in part as an adjunct of landscape architecture in the 1920's, as were later academic courses in urban design) now boasts thirty-seven schools. Such schools are a direct result of the efforts of men trained by Olmsted.

We could say that planning for American physical development alternates in its concern between long-range and short-range needs. Faced with a birth rate that will increase population more rapidly than all past immigrations, we are again beginning to focus on the needs of future generations. Among present efforts are the promotion of new towns, a renewed interest in public preserves such as Cape Cod's seashore, total urban design schemes such as Hartford's Constitution Plaza, and public action in some cities such as San Francisco to ensure design focus on natural assets. In such projects it is perhaps Olmsted's example that is most relevant.

His character combined a deep love of nature with a commitment to hard work and social service. To these traits he added organizational talent, keen observation, attention to detail, skills as a publicist, and the courage to define the scope of his projects and promote them despite opposition from less far-sighted associates. It is precisely these traits that today's designers will need in the execution of their long-range projects.

Appendix I

Significant Works of Olmsted

The most significant professional design work of Frederick Law Olmsted, Sr. and his partners is listed below. This information is summarized from *Forty Years of Landscape Architecture* and from his office portfolio. We have deliberately grouped his works under contemporary categories such as "Urban Design" and "Regional Design" in order to compare Olmsted's work with that of his modern counterparts. In most instances the duties indicated for a work show its major design and construction phases; Olmsted's firm often served as a permanent consultant on design and maintenance problems after such work had been completed.

URBAN PARKS

Central Park, New York City   1858–ca. 1880
Prospect Park, Brooklyn, New York   1865–1888
Public Pleasure Grounds for San Francisco, California   1866–1868
Fort Green Park, Brooklyn, New York   1867
Park for New Britain, Connecticut   1867–1870
Park for Newark, New Jersey   1867
City Park for Albany, New York   1868
Parks for Hartford, Connecticut   1870–1895
Park for Fall River, Massachusetts   1870
South Park, Chicago, Illinois   1871
Park in Philadelphia, Pennsylvania   1871
Mount Royal, Montreal, Quebec   1873–1881
Common, Amherst, Massachusetts   1874
Amusement resort, Rockaway Point, New York   1879
Belle Isle Park, Detroit, Michigan   1882–1883
South Park, Buffalo, New York   1882–1893
Beardsley Park, Bridgeport, Connecticut   1882–1886
Memorial Park, New London, Connecticut   1884
Park for Trenton, New Jersey   1884
Riverside Park, New York City   1886

[103]

Franklin Park, Boston, Massachusetts   1886
Morningside Park, New York City   1887
National Zoo at Washington, D.C.   1887–1893
Seneca Park, Rochester, New York   1887–1893
Park system, Pawtucket, Rhode Island   1888
Wood Island Park, Boston, Massachusetts   1889–1891
Charlestown Playground, Boston, Massachusetts   1891
Washington Park, Albany, New York   1891–1895
Boone Square, Louisville, Kentucky   1892
Logan Place, Louisville, Kentucky   1892
Kenton Place, Louisville, Kentucky   1892
Bay Ridge Parkway, New York City   1893–1895
Park for Louisville, Kentucky   1893
Park for Kansas City, Missouri   1893
Lake Park, Milwaukee, Wisconsin   1893–1895
West Park, Milwaukee, Wisconsin   1895
Jackson Park, Chicago, Illinois   1895

COMMUNITY DESIGN

Riverside near Chicago, Illinois   1868–1869
Tarrytown Heights subdivision, New York   1871–1872
"Belleview" suburb of Newark, New Jersey   1879
Providence subdivision, Rhode Island   1882
Aspinwall Land Company subdivision, Summit, New Jersey   1882
Providence land subdivision, Rhode Island   1882
Goddard land subdivision, Providence, Rhode Island   1883
Chestnut Hill subdivision, Massachusetts   1884–1888
Newport & Providence, Rhode Island; Yonkers, New York   1884–1888
Newport Hospital subdivision, Rhode Island   1886
Six subdivisions in Brookline, Massachusetts   1886–1888
Swampscott, Massachusetts subdivision   1888
Buffalo subdivisions, New York   1888
Sudbrook, Baltimore, Maryland   1889
"World's End" development, Boston Harbor, Massachusetts   1889
Kirkwood Land Company, Atlanta, Georgia   1893

ESTATES

Mr. Lord, Morristown, New Jersey   1874
Weld Estate at Dedham, Massachusetts   1882
H. H. Hunnewel Estate at Wellesley, Massachusetts   1882
Biltmore Estate for Mr. George W. Vanderbilt, Asheville, North Carolina   1888–1893

URBAN DESIGN

World's Columbian Exposition, Chicago, Illinois   1890–1893

INSTITUTIONAL WORKS

Massachusetts General Hospital, Boston, Massachusetts   1872
Oakwood Cemetery, Syracuse, New York   1874
Hartford Insane Retreat, Hartford, Connecticut   1874
Schuylkill Arsenal, Philadelphia, Pennsylvania   1875
McLean Asylum, Waverly, Massachusetts   1875–1886
New Capitol at Albany, New York   1876–1882
Buffalo State Asylum, Buffalo, New York   1876
Connecticut State Capitol, Hartford, Connecticut   1878
Boston and Albany Railroad Stations   1883–1885
Capitol Grounds and Lafayette Square, Washington, D.C.   1874–1885

CAMPUS DESIGN

Estate of the College of California at Berkeley, California   1866
Amherst College, Amherst, Massachusetts   1870–1885
Trinity College, Hartford, Connecticut   1872–1893
Yale College, New Haven, Connecticut   1874
Johns Hopkins University, Baltimore, Maryland   1874–1876
Madison (now Colgate) University, Hamilton, New York   1883
University of Vermont, Burlington, Vermont   1884
Smith College, Northampton, Massachusetts   1885
Harvard University, Cambridge, Massachusetts   1886
Stanford University, Stanford, California   1886–1889
University at Palo Alto, California   1886
United States Military Academy, West Point, New York   1890
College of New Jersey, Princeton, New Jersey   1893
Washington University, St. Louis, Missouri   1895

CONSERVATION WORKS

Mariposa Mining Estates in California   1863
Yosemite and Mariposa Big Tree Groves, California   1864
Niagara Falls, New York   1869–1885

REGIONAL DESIGN

Boston Park System, Boston, Massachusetts and surrounding communities
    1875–1895
The parts of the system in which he actively participated are as follows:

Franklin Park	Charles River Embankment
Arborway	Parkway, Five Corners to Marine Park
Arnold Arboretum	Marine Park
Jamaica Park	Bay Ridge Parkway in Brookline
Leverett Park	Blue Hills Parkway
Jamaicaway	Mystic Valley Parkway
Riverway	Middlesex Fells Parkway
Fenway, The Fens	Revere Beach Reservation
Commonwealth Avenue	Charles River Reservation

Appendix II

Important Dates in Olmsted's Life

1822   APRIL 26: Born at Hartford, Connecticut of Charlotte Law (Hull) and John Olmsted.

1826–1836   At various boarding schools in Connecticut preparing for college.

1837   Advised to give up college on account of weak eyes.
NOVEMBER: Went to Andover, Massachusetts to study engineering with a Professor Barton. (November 1838, Barton removed to Collinsville, Connecticut and Frederick with him; stayed until May 1840.)

1840   AUGUST: Went to work for Benkard and Hutton, French dry-goods importers, New York City. (Left their employ March 1842.)

1842   Attended lectures at Yale.

1843   APRIL: Sailed before the mast for Canton in the bark "Rolandson." (Vessel back in New York April 1844.)

1844–1847   Studying farming in Connecticut and New York.

1847   JUNE: An honorary member of the Class of 1847 at Yale.

1848   JANUARY: Father bought for Frederick the Ackerly Farm, Staten Island, New York, which he continued to operate until 1854.

1850   APRIL to OCTOBER: Traveling in Europe and the British Isles.

1851   Visited Andrew Jackson Downing at Newburgh, New York.

1852   FEBRUARY: Published *Walks and Talks of an American Farmer in England.*
DECEMBER: Started on Southern tour.

1853   FEBRUARY: Letters to the New York *Times* began, giving his impressions of the "Seabord Slave States."
NOVEMBER: Frederick and his brother John started on journey to Mexico and California; Frederick again as correspondent to the *Times.*

1855   With G. W. Curtis went into partnership with Dix and Edwards in publishing

[107]

business. Edited *Putnam's Magazine*. Publishing business failed in 1856.

1856   Traveling in Europe.

1857   SEPTEMBER: Appointed Superintendent of Central Park in New York.

1857–1858   Collaborated with Calvert Vaux in the preparation of a design for Central Park to submit in the competition—"Greensward."

1858   APRIL: Olmsted and Vaux awarded first prize for their plan, "Greensward."
            MAY: Appointed Architect in Chief of Central Park.

1859   JUNE: Married Mary Cleveland (Perkins) Olmsted, widow of his brother John Hull Olmsted.
            SEPTEMBER to DECEMBER: Traveling in Europe.

1860   Furnished to Appleton's *New American Cyclopedia* first article on "Parks" in any American encyclopedia.
            APRIL: Olmsted and Vaux appointed "Landscape Architects and Designers to the Commissioners North of 155th Street," New York City.

1861   *Journeys and Explorations in the Cotton Kingdom* published in London, a compilation of three previous volumes on his Southern journeys.
            JUNE: Leave of absence granted to go to Washington as Secretary of the United States Sanitary Commission of which he was chief executive officer until 1863; connection with Central Park still retained.

1862   Offered office of Street Commissioner of New York; accepted but not consummated.

1862–1863   Joined with Dr. Bellows, Wolcott Gibbs, and others in formation of the Union League Club to perpetuate the ideals of the United States Sanitary Commission.

1863   MAY: Olmsted and Vaux resigned as Landscape Architects of Central Park.
            SUMMER: Obliged to withdraw from Sanitary Commission owing to overwork. Interested with C. E. Norton and others in founding a weekly review; this project developed into *The Nation*.
            AUGUST: Offered superintendency of the Mariposa Mining Estates in California. Accepted; arrived in San Francisco in October.

1864   SPRING: Honorary A.M. from Harvard University for his work on the United States Sanitary Commission.
            SEPTEMBER: Appointed Commissioner of Yosemite and Mariposa Big Tree Grove by Governor of California.

[108]

1865   MARCH: Preliminary reconnoissance for a large piece of ground held by the College of California (later the University of California at Berkeley).
JULY: Offered work on *The Nation*. Olmsted and Vaux reappointed Landscape Architects to the Board of Commissioners of Central Park.
FALL: Accepts Central Park appointment and resigns from Mariposa Estates. Advising on park for San Francisco. Olmsted and Vaux appointed to design the Brooklyn (Prospect) Park.

1866   Work on Prospect Park.

1867   SPRING: Honorary A.M. Amherst College.
JUNE: Advice to C. E. Norton on grounds and property of Harvard University (also in 1868, 1869, and later).

1868   Preliminary report on the proposed suburban village at Riverside near Chicago.

1869   Brooklyn Park and Riverside going on.
SEPTEMBER: Meeting regarding the preservation of Niagara Falls.

1870   Address before the American Social Science Association: "Public Parks and the Enlargement of Towns."
NOVEMBER: Olmsted and Vaux resigned from Central Park after their advice had been disregarded.

1871   NOVEMBER: Olmsted and Vaux reappointed Landscape Architects of New York Department of Public Parks.

1872   OCTOBER: Partnership between Olmsted and Vaux dissolved.

1873   Active work on Central Park, preparation of a large number of special reports. Preliminary visit to Mount Royal, Montreal.

1874   Report submitted on public grounds at Washington, including Capitol Grounds and area to Lafayette Square.
NOVEMBER: Engaged for advice on Mount Royal Park and furnished written instructions during construction (1874–1876).

1875–1877   Various park work throughout the country.

1878   JANUARY: Sailed for Europe for four months.
FEBRUARY: Dismissed from Central Park.
DECEMBER: Memorial for preservation of Niagara Falls. Signs articles of agreement with Park Department of Boston in regard to "Back Bay Park."

1879	OCTOBER: Meets New York State Niagara Commissioners and members of the Council of Ontario; his general scheme approved.
1880	Reads paper at the meeting of the American Social Science Association: "A Consideration of the Justifying Value of a Small Park."
1881	Work for Boston Parks proceeding.
1882	FEBRUARY: Published "Spoils of the Park," an account of political interference in the management of Central Park.
1883	Permanent home and office in Brookline, Massachusetts. Successful conclusion of campaign for the preservation of Niagara Falls.
1884–1885	Work in and around Boston going on.
1886	Report: "Notes on the Plan of Franklin Park [Boston]. . . ." Begins work on Stanford University.
1887	Work in Boston and New York.
1888	AUGUST: Preliminary discussion for Biltmore Estate for George W. Vanderbilt at Asheville, North Carolina.
1889	Report on Central Park: "Observations on the Treatment of Public Plantations."
1890	Collection of United States Sanitary Commission Papers arranged and presented by Olmsted to the Loyal Legion of Boston. JUNE: Report: "Project of Operations for the Improvement of the Forest of Biltmore" sent to Vanderbilt. AUGUST: In Chicago reporting on a site for the World's Fair.
1891	Chicago and Biltmore claimed the major part of his time.
1892	APRIL: Sailed for Europe for rest. OCTOBER: In Chicago on World's Fair business; present at dedication ceremonies of the Fair and received one of the special medals for the architects, artists, and designers of the World's Columbian Exposition. NOVEMBER: At Biltmore for conference with Vanderbilt.
1893	JANUARY: Sudden death of Harry Codman made it necessary for Olmsted to take over the World's Fair work. FEBRUARY: From this time on he declined personal responsibility for all private work except Biltmore which he considered semi-public.

MARCH: Guest of honor at a dinner given for the artists of
the Columbian Exposition by fellow architects and the City of New York.
JUNE: LL.D. from Harvard and also from Yale.

1894   Occupied with work on Biltmore.

1895   SEPTEMBER: Retired from professional practice.
              NOVEMBER: Sailed for England.
              DECEMBER: His mind failed after nearly forty years of active work.

1895–1903   Resting at McLean Asylum, Waverley, Massachusetts.

1903   AUGUST 28: Died.

Summarized from the Biographical Notes in *Forty Years of Landscape Architecture.*

Bibliography

Important Writings of Frederick Law Olmsted, Sr.

See also the annual reports and published documents of the Commissioners of Central Park, the United States Sanitary Commission, the Brooklyn Park Commission the New York Park Department, and the Boston Park Department.

Books and Printed Papers Relating to the Concerns of the United States Sanitary Commission . . ., Boston, 1890.

A Consideration of the Justifying Value of a Public Park, Boston, 1881.

The Cotton Kingdom; a Traveler's Observations on Cotton and Slavery in the American Slave States, 2 vols., New York, 1861.

Description of a Plan for the Improvement of the Central Park, "Greensward," New York, 1856 (reprinted 1868).

Effect of Secession upon the Commercial Relation Between the North and South, New York, 1861.

A Few Things to be Thought of Before Proceeding to Plan Buildings for the National Agricultural Colleges, New York, 1866.

Frederick Law Olmsted, Landscape Architect: Forty Years of Landscape Architecture, 2 vols., ed. F. L. Olmsted, Jr. and T. Kimball, New York and London, 1922–1928.

General Plan for the Improvement of Niagara Reservation, Albany, 1887.

"George W. Vanderbilt's Nursery," *Lyceum* II, 6, 1891.

Hospital Transports; a Memoir of the Embarkation of the Sick and Wounded from the Peninsula of Virginia in the Summer of 1862, Boston, 1863.

"Introduction" to *The Englishman in Kansas . . .*, by Thomas H. Gladstone, New York, 1857.

A Journey in the Back Country, New York and London, 1860.

A Journey in the Seaboard Slave States, New York and London, 1856.

A Journey Through Texas; or a Saddle-trip on the Southwestern Frontier, New York and London, 1857.

Journeys and Explorations in the Cotton Kingdom, 2 vols., London, 1861.

"Landscape Gardening," *Johnson's Encyclopedia*, New York, 1877.

Mariposa Estate: Manager's General Report, New York, 1864.

"Notes on Niagara Falls," *Special Report on the Preservation of Niagara Falls*, Albany, New York, 1880.

Notes on the Plan of Franklin Park and Related Matters, Boston, 1886.

Observations on the Treatment of Public Plantations, Boston, 1889.

"Parks," *Appleton's New American Cyclopedia*, New York, 1861 (revised 1875).

Preliminary Report Respecting a Public Park in Buffalo . . ., Buffalo, 1869.

Preliminary Report Upon the Proposed Suburban Village at Riverside, Near Chicago, New York, 1868.

Public Parks and the Enlargement of Towns, Cambridge, Massachusetts, 1870.

Report Upon a Projected Improvement of the Estate of the College of California at Berkeley, Near Oakland, New York, 1866.

"Report upon the Landscape Architecture of the Columbian Exposition," *American Architect and Building News*, September, 1893.

Spoils of the Park, New York, 1882.

Walks and Talks of an American Farmer in England, New York and London, 1852.

Walks and Talks of an American Farmer in England, new edition with additions, Columbus, Ohio, 1859.